YOUR SINS ARE FORGIVEN YOU

*Dedicated to*

DR. PETER KAY

*who uses his healing gifts*
*to reconcile many*
*to the Source of all Beauty*

# YOUR SINS ARE FORGIVEN YOU

### Rediscovering the
### SACRAMENT OF RECONCILIATION

## GEORGE A. MALONEY, SJ

ALBA·HOUSE    NEW·YORK

SOCIETY OF ST. PAUL, 2187 VICTORY BLVD., STATEN ISLAND, NEW YORK 10314

Library of Congress Cataloging-in-Publication Data

Maloney, George A., 1924-
    Your sins are forgiven you: rediscovering the sacrament of
reconciliation / George A. Maloney.
        p.    cm.
    Includes bibliographical references.
    ISBN 0-8189-0691-X
    1. Reconciliation — Religious aspects — Catholic Church.
    2. Penance. 3. Forgiveness of sin — History of doctrines.
    I. Title.
    BX2260.M32    1994
    234'.166 — dc20                          93-43836
                                                CIP


Imprimi Potest:
Rev. Albert Thelen, S.J.
Provincial of the Wisconsin Province
   of the Society of Jesus
July 6, 1993

---

Produced and designed in the United States of America by the
Fathers and Brothers of the Society of St. Paul,
2187 Victory Boulevard, Staten Island, New York 10314,
as part of their communications apostolate.


ISBN: 0-8189-0691-X

---

---

**Printing Information:**

| Current Printing - first digit | 1 | 2 | 3 | 4 | 5 | 6 | 7 | 8 | 9 | 10 |
|---|---|---|---|---|---|---|---|---|---|---|

Year of Current Printing - first year shown

| 1994 | 1995 | 1996 | 1997 | 1998 | 1999 |
|---|---|---|---|---|---|

# CONTENTS

INTRODUCTION ...................................................................................... xi

A Difficult Sacrament to Receive ........................................... xi
The Purpose of this Book ........................................................ xii
Sinfulness, Repentance and Conversion .............................. xiii
Apostolic and Patristic Writings ........................................... xiii
Development of Private Confession ...................................... xiii
New Rites of Reconciliation .................................................. xiv
Elements of Communal Penance Services ............................ xiv

CHAPTER 1: WHY HAVE SO MANY CATHOLICS STOPPED
              GOING TO CONFESSION? ...................................... 1

Early Memories ......................................................................... 1
Historical Research on the Sacrament of Penance .............. 3
General Dissatisfaction ........................................................... 3
No Longer Meaningful ............................................................ 4
The New Rite ............................................................................ 4
Loss of a Sense of Sin ............................................................. 5
Sense of Sin .............................................................................. 6
To Sin Is to Miss the Mark ..................................................... 8
Legalistic Approach and Magical Tendencies ...................... 8
Unhealthy Elements ................................................................ 9
A New Rite Not So New! ......................................................... 10
These three ways or Rites are: ............................................... 10
The Centrality of Private Absolution .................................... 11
Mortal and Venial Sins ........................................................... 11
A Blurring of Distinctions ...................................................... 12
Dawning of a New Awareness ................................................ 12

CHAPTER 2: HUMAN SINFULNESS, REPENTANCE
AND CONVERSION ...................................................15

The Gold of the Holy Spirit.................................................15
Restless Searchings of the Human Heart .....................16
Human Sinfulness................................................................17
The Dynamics of Sin .........................................................18
Sin and Repentance ...........................................................18
The Ritual of Repentance ..................................................19
Confession ............................................................................20
Judaism ..................................................................................20
Claiming One's Sinfulness ................................................21
Remembrance of Sins of the Past ...................................22
The Experience of Personal Sins .....................................22
The Sanctity of the People of God...................................23
Faith of the Patriarchs and Prophets .............................24
Two Ways ..............................................................................24
A New Enlightenment ........................................................25

CHAPTER 3: JESUS: THE LIVING SACRAMENT OF GOD'S
MERCIFUL RECONCILIATION ..........................................27

Jesus, Living and Active .....................................................27
Jesus, The Healing Light ....................................................27
The Message of Reconciliation ........................................28
The Poor Have the Gospel Preached to Them ..............29
Metanoia ................................................................................29
Jesus Speaks of God's Forgiving Mercy .......................30
Jesus Speaks of God's Forgiving Love ..........................31
Jesus Teaches Mercy and Reconciliation ......................31
Jesus Spoke in Parables ....................................................32
The Prodigal Father ............................................................32
A Rejoicing Father Who Forgives Sinners....................33
A Waiting God.......................................................................34
Jesus Acts as Reconciler of the Father ...........................35
Fullness of Mercy and Reconciliation on the Cross....36
Death and Resurrection .....................................................36
The Glory of the Cross, Our Reconciling Hope ...........38
Paradoxes in Christianity ..................................................38

# Contents

Christ's Church: Another Sacrament of Reconciliation .............. 39
Shared Authority ..................................................................... 40
Jesus Risen Is Still Present Through Shared Authority ............. 41
Tradition and Traditions ............................................................ 41
Conclusion .................................................................................. 43

CHAPTER 4: THE SACRAMENT OF RECONCILIATION IN THE
         APOSTOLIC AND PATRISTIC CHURCHES ...................... 45

The Evolution of a Sacrament ..................................................... 45
Jesus Ministered God's Reconciliation ..................................... 46
Shared Power in Forgiving Sins ................................................ 46
The Church Community as Sacrament of Reconciliation .......... 48
The Separation and Correction of Grave Sinners ....................... 49
The Power of Excommunication ................................................. 49
Confession of Sins ...................................................................... 50
Submission to Leaders of the Church ....................................... 51
The Shepherd of Hermas ............................................................ 53
Elements of a Penitential Rite Appear ...................................... 54
Apostasy and Martyrdom ........................................................... 57
Gradual Reform .......................................................................... 58

CHAPTER 5: DEVELOPMENT OF PRIVATE CONFESSION .............. 61

The Mediterranean Form of Reconciliation ............................... 61
Development of the Celtic Form of Reconciliation ..................... 62
A Monastic Church ..................................................................... 62
Spiritual Direction in the Desert ............................................... 63
Eastern Churches and Monastic Influences .............................. 64
Celtic Form of Reconciliation .................................................... 64
Commutation of Penances .......................................................... 65
Penance, a Catechetical Tool ..................................................... 66
Disadvantages of the Celtic Form of Confession ...................... 67
Good Friday Rites ....................................................................... 67
Tensions and Clashes Between the Two Forms
    of Reconciliation .................................................................... 68
Reforms of the Fourth Lateran Council (1215) ........................... 69
Importance of Priestly Absolution ............................................ 70
The Formula of Absolution ........................................................ 71

The Effects of the Council of Trent on Confession ...................... 72
The Confession of Venial Sins ............................................. 73
From Trent to Vatican II ................................................. 73

CHAPTER 6: NEW RITES FOR RECEIVING THE SACRAMENT
  OF RECONCILIATION ...................................................... 75

The Emergence of New Rituals ............................................. 75
Vatican II Mandates ...................................................... 76
Ecclesial Aspects of the Sacrament Rediscovered ....................... 76
Ordo Penitentiae ......................................................... 78
New Formulas of Absolution ............................................... 78
Declarative Formula of Absolution ....................................... 80
Rite I: Reconciliation of Individual Penitents ......................... 80
Rite II: Reconciliation of Several Penitents with
  Individual Confession and Absolution ................................. 83
Difficulties Created by Rite II .......................................... 84
Rite III: Reconciliation of Penitents with General Absolution .... 85
Celebration of Rite III .................................................. 85
Summary and Conclusions .................................................. 86

CHAPTER 7: COMMUNAL SERVICE OF RECONCILIATION ............. 89

A State of General Confusion ............................................. 89
Lack of Implementation ................................................... 90
Norms Issued by the Vatican .............................................. 90
Present State of the Sacrament ........................................... 91
Different Needs Demand Different Rituals ................................. 92
Non-Sacramental Means of Reconciliation ................................. 93
Healing of Memories ...................................................... 94
Examination of Conscience ................................................ 94
Communal Penance Services for Children ................................... 95
Two Forms of Reconciliation .............................................. 97
Problems Associated with Both Forms ...................................... 97

CHAPTER 8: THE CELEBRATION OF COMMUNAL
  PENANCE SERVICES ........................................................ 99

True Repentance and the Holy Spirit ...................................... 99
History of Communal Penance Services .................................... 100

## Contents

The Church's Role in Reconciliation ........................................... 101
A Suggested Form of Communal Reconciliation ..................... 102
Format of the Celebration ......................................................... 102
Explanation ................................................................................ 103
A Communal Healing and Penance Service ............................. 104
   A. Examen According to the Eight Beatitudes ...................... 104
   B. Penitential Litany ............................................................. 107
The Liturgy of the Word ........................................................... 110
Reverse Creation ....................................................................... 110
The Liturgy of the Eucharist .................................................... 112

CHAPTER 9: THE SACRAMENT OF RECONCILIATION AMONG
           EASTERN ORTHODOX CHRISTIANS TODAY ............... 113

Orthodox Practice ..................................................................... 113
Infrequent Reception of the Eucharist ..................................... 114
The Minister of the Sacrament ................................................. 114
Integrity of One's Confession ................................................... 115
Different Forms of Celebration Within the Community ........... 116
Communal Reconciliation Service and General Absolution ...... 116
Community Forgiveness ............................................................. 119
Conclusion ................................................................................. 120

NOTES .............................................................................................. 121

# INTRODUCTION

## A Difficult Sacrament to Receive

Of all the seven sacraments in the Roman Catholic and Orthodox Churches, the Sacrament of Reconciliation is the most difficult one for us to receive. It will always be hard for us to manifest to any human being, especially to a priest, our failures and sins, the dark side of our personality.

Catholics are not receiving this sacrament as frequently as they did before Vatican II. Part of this is due to the radical change in our thinking about God, the Church, and ourselves since the Council. For many of us, confession involved a long list of sins repeated by rote, neatly tabulated according to kind and number, and told to the priest in order to be absolved from them.

Many of us realize that we do not have an adequate sense of sin and we feel uneasy about going to confession because we recognize that we do not know ourselves deeply enough to be in touch with what St. Paul called the "sin which lives within me" (Rm 7:20). But we do know that the "grocery list" we have repeated in our past confessions does not have much to do with our existential situation. Still we don't quite know what to tell the priest, or how to approach this sacrament in a more meaningful and personal way.

This impersonal and legalistic approach to confession has hindered much true repentance and lessened its effectiveness as a personalized encounter with God's deep love and mercy. Under ordinary circumstances, it does not really touch us deeply enough to fill us with genuine sorrow for our sins, nor does it move us to a true change in our everyday life. Our faith, though, assures us that Jesus, our Lord and Reconciler, is always ready to lead us to a deeper conversion if we but ask him for this grace.

## The Purpose of this Book

I have done a lot of research lately into the many convolutions and changes in the Sacrament of Reconciliation over the centuries. Especially since Vatican Council II, many modern scholars have written important works on the evolution of this sacrament. These have been studied extensively and are quoted by me in this book as are other works written by contemporary liturgists and "practical" theologians.

This book is a pastoral attempt to stir Christians to see the need for individual and communal renewal in an ongoing conversion grounded on deep repentance and a genuine change in their lives.

We cannot understand the power of the Sacrament of Reconciliation to effect such a renewal under the power of the Holy Spirit unless we understand something of its history. Down through the ages, the Holy Spirit has been at work evolving the insights of the Church and developing effective liturgical rituals to signify and to bring about a true encounter with the primordial Sacrament of Reconciliation, Jesus Christ, our Lord. Just as an acorn in some potential way already contains the full oak tree in embryonic form, so the early practices of the Church with respect to the Sacrament of Reconciliation reveal in embryonic form the characteristics we see today in the various forms of its celebration.

## *Sinfulness, Repentance and Conversion*

We need to begin by exploring our human sinfulness and the need we all have to call out to the Savior to forgive, reconcile and heal us. This process of conversion goes on throughout the whole of our earthly life. We must study the essential elements of repentance if we are to renew our appreciation and effective reception of the Sacrament of Reconciliation. Before we can suggest how this sacrament can be renewed, we need to be grounded in Christ Jesus, the primordial Sacrament of Reconciliation as revealed in the New Testament and encountered through the Church. Therefore, in Chapter Three we establish through an authentic Christology and ecclesiology that Jesus is still reconciling us to the Father through his Holy Spirit just as he did in his life on earth.

## *Apostolic and Patristic Writings*

To understand the rituals we have inherited, we must study the beginnings of this sacrament as revealed in the life of the early Christian Church and described in the apostolic and patristic writings of the first three centuries. In these early writings, we see Jesus' power to reconcile sinners to the heavenly Father passed down through the first apostles and their early successors, the bishops. And we also note how both the leaders and the members of the early communities were mutually involved in this exercise of reconciliation.

## *Development of Private Confession*

From the 5th century on, through the influence of the Celtic missionary-monks and bishops there developed a new, popular form of receiving the Sacrament of Penance. This was through the use of private confession that spread from northern Europe to influence the Western Roman Church from that time to the present. The Fourth Lateran Council in 1215 promoted private confession as the ordinary way to have serious sins forgiven and extolled it as a useful means for obtaining spiritual direction on the part of those who wished to grow in perfection.

## New Rites of Reconciliation

Vatican Council II recommended a reform of this sacrament and emphasized communal participation within the Church community. This led to the promulgation of the New Rite in 1973 (1975 in the U.S.A.). Chapters Six through Eight examine in detail the three forms for celebrating the Sacrament of Reconciliation. These chapters describe the importance and richness found in each of these three forms, while at the same time they discuss some of the difficulties the forms present which have gotten in the way of a realistic renewal in the lives of average Catholics. Private confession according to Form I and the communal penance service with general confession and absolution of Form III are presented as complementary and authentic forms of validly receiving this sacrament.

## Elements of Communal Penance Services

Since not much has been written on communal services of reconciliation, I have taken pains to develop this important topic at some length. The Holy Spirit in our day has given us two complementary forms of celebrating our reconciliation with God and with the Church, and we penitents can freely choose that form which seems better suited to help us attain a deeper sense of sorrow for our sins, and a firmer resolve to avoid them in the future; in other words, we are free to choose that form which will more effectively assist our conversion to a more dynamic and holy Christian life.

I include, therefore, two items which I hope will be helpful: an example of a communal penance service at the end of Chapter Eight; and an overview of the modern state of this sacrament among the Eastern Orthodox Christians in Chapter Nine.

I humbly pray that, under the guidance of the Holy Spirit, this book will contribute to a widespread rediscovery of the great gift of the Sacrament of Reconciliation and that those who read it will be open to a more personal, more fruitful encounter with the living Lord who meets us in this sacrament to heal us of our brokenness and forgive us all our sins.

*Feast of Pentecost*

Chapter One

# WHY HAVE SO MANY CATHOLICS STOPPED GOING TO CONFESSION?

*Early Memories*

When I was in the second grade and all of seven years old, I made my first confession. Unlike most Catholics, I rather liked going to confession. For a year or so, I went regularly each Saturday. My mother asked me each Saturday what I was telling the priest. "That's between me and God," I would reply as I guarded my sacred "sins." To this day, I wonder why I so enjoyed going to confession when most other Catholics I knew, including my own brothers and sister and classmates, hated the ordeal.

I guess I enjoyed that "clean" feeling that came over me when I left the confessional box and said my three Hail Marys. God had forgiven me my sins, and I was at peace with God and the entire world. I am sure I had a very primitive, childlike understanding of sin. But one thing was certain from early childhood until now: Jesus Christ had given his Church the power to proclaim God's healing and forgiving mercy to all who came and humbly opened up their inner sinfulness to his infinite, triune love.

The new *Catechism of the Catholic Church* refers to the various names that have been given to this sacrament. "It is called the *sacrament of conversion* because it sacramentally fulfills Jesus' invitation to conversion (cf. Mk 1:15), a return to the Father (cf. Lk 15:18) from whom man has estranged himself through sin. It is called the *sacrament of penance* because it makes holy a personal and ecclesial process of conversion, of repentance and reparation on the part of the Christian who is a sinner. It is called the *sacrament of confession* because the declaration or manifestation, the confession of sins before a priest, is an essential element of this sacrament. In a profound sense this sacrament is also a 'confession,' an acknowledgment and praise of the holiness of God and of his mercy toward sinful human beings. It is called the *sacrament of forgiveness* because, through the sacramental absolution of the priest, God grants to the penitent 'pardon and peace.' It is called the *sacrament of reconciliation* because it confers on the sinner the love of God who reconciles. 'Be reconciled to God' (2 Cor 5:20). Whoever lives in the merciful love of God will be prompt to respond to the invitation of the Lord: 'Go first and be reconciled with your brother' (Mt 5:24)" (*Catechism of the Catholic Church*, October 22, 1992, #1423 & #1424).

Of all the Church's sacraments, the Sacrament of Confession or Reconciliation is the one that has undergone the greatest, most diverse developments over the centuries, both in the Eastern and Western Churches. Above all, this sacrament is the most difficult for us to receive. We do not need pollsters to tell us that we do not frequent this sacrament as often as we did in pre-Vatican II times. We feel uneasy and we suspect that there is something missing, at least in the manner in which we go to confession.

In spite of the new Rite promulgated in 1973, the majority of Catholics, clerics, religious, and laity no longer go to confession on any regular basis. Priests in parishes agree that the Sacrament of Reconciliation for most Catholics is dying out as an important encounter with Christ.

The Roman Catholic Church is undergoing a new period in the evolution of the sacrament and people are finding it hard to adjust. From the exclusive ritual of private confession before a priest, we now have in addition the use of communal penance services, with or without private confession before a priest as a part of the service.

Vatican Council II decreed in its *Constitution on the Sacred Liturgy:*

> The rite and formulas for the Sacrament of Penance are to be revised so that they give more luminous expression to both the nature and effect of the sacrament.[1]

## Historical Research on the Sacrament of Penance

A great deal of historical research and writing has been done recently in the areas of sacramental theology and ecclesiology to relate the sacramental signs in their ecclesial, communitarian dimensions to the scriptural signs of salvation.[2]

A study of the history of dogma and related liturgical practices has made us acutely aware of the growth that has taken place down through the ages in both areas in the Eastern and Western Churches. With this in mind, we intend to examine in this chapter some of the reasons why many Catholics no longer see the Sacrament of Reconciliation as playing an important role in their spiritual life, at least in the historical forms inherited from the Council of Trent (1551).

## General Dissatisfaction

Most Catholics, especially younger Catholics, do not go to confession regularly. This is obviously not because Catholics are becoming holier and are sinning less than they did a few decades ago. The reason would seem to lie in the general dissatisfaction that many feel about the way in which they receive this sacrament. Much in the ritual of private confession to a priest seems irrelevant to many of them. They have been discovering that the way the sacrament is being administered, even with the new Rite of Reconciliation,[3] has little to do with their "real life" situations. Too often, they have assumed that some magical effect would take place by going through a prescribed ritual (either before a priest in the dark anonymity of the confessional box or in the lighted, spacious reconciliation

3

room), usually confessing a memorized and oft-repeated grocery list of sins. When that effect does not seem to take place, they are disappointed.

Frequent confession declined in most parishes and religious orders when Catholics began to question what the sins they were confessing had to do with the life they led here on earth or the one they hoped to lead in heaven. The concept of sin inherited from the Council of Trent seemed too impersonal and legalistic to be meaningful. Catholics began to feel that numbering their transgressions against an impersonal law no longer provided, if it ever did, a true picture of who they really were before God, neighbor, and the world around them.

## No Longer Meaningful

Yet they were given no other way to determine their sinfulness than to be guided by lists of sins which followed the ten commandments. This stereotyped, almost mechanical type of confession, did not give a true picture of what they needed for true conversion. Going regularly to confession did not seem to be bringing them to the point where they were experiencing God's goodness as healing and forgiving love. Nor were they being taught by their priest-confessors how to get in touch more deeply with the false ego within themselves. They were not given a more scriptural and existential sense of their sinfulness.

## The New Rite

The Vatican Congregation for Divine Worship promulgated the new Rite of Penance on December 2, 1973. It was implemented in all parishes in the United States by the first Sunday of Lent, 1975. This sacrament was now to be called the Sacrament of Reconciliation rather than Penance or Confession since it was felt that this term better captured both the idea of God's initiative and that of our response to his saving love. The new Rite changed some of the externals and made the encounter between priest and penitent more personal, meaningful and loving.

Still crowds did not return to the sacrament. They had not been instructed in the deeper root of the problem: a genuine understanding of sin and the need for reconciliation. By our sin we find ourselves estranged from God, from ourselves and from our ecclesial community. All this needs to be righted and healed. Since the promulgation of the new Rite there is an urgent need for an effective catechesis in this area.

We can agree with John McIlhon that among those who continue to frequent the sacrament, there are two classes. The first class of penitents are the "grocery-listers" who follow the ritual and practices handed down from the Council of Trent[4] which taught that, to obtain absolution from mortal sins, they must all be confessed in number and kind. Venial sins may likewise be confessed in the same manner though there is no obligation to do so. These people generally go to confession out of a desire to receive greater grace and attain a higher place for themselves in heaven. Their approach is probably more of the head than of the heart.

The second class of penitents consists of those who have entered into a new stage in their personal relationship with Jesus possibly as a result of a Cursillo, Marriage Encounter, the Charismatic Renewal, adult education, Renew or other parish-oriented renewal program. They tend to experience their sinfulness as a personal alienation from Jesus and sense an urgent need for healing the roots of their self-centeredness in their approach to this sacrament, which is usually more of the heart than of the head.

## Loss of a Sense of Sin

In our society sin has almost completely disappeared from the vocabulary and everyday experience of the average person. Many have difficulty understanding the difference between good and evil, right and wrong. Indeed, society often calls what was at one time considered inherently wrong, good and ridicules what was once considered good as evil. All kinds of excuses are at hand to explain the wrong we do: we came from a dysfunctional family, we are undergoing an identity crisis, the devil made me do it. Rarely do we take full responsibility for the sin in our lives. And, failing to acknowledge the presence of sin, we can hardly be expected to see the need to confess it. The Sacrament of Reconciliation is thus easily relegated to the museum of quaint but outmoded practices of a bygone age.

In his best-selling book, *Whatever Became of Sin?*, Dr. Karl Menninger wrote:

In all of the laments and reproaches made by our seers and prophets, one misses any mention of "sin," a word which used to be a veritable watchword of prophets. It was a word more in everyone's mind, but now rarely if ever heard. Does that mean that no sin is involved in all our troubles — sin with an "I" in the middle? Is no one any longer guilty of anything? Guilty perhaps of a sin that could be repented and repaired or atoned for? Is it only that someone may be stupid or sick or criminal, or asleep? Wrong things are being done, we know. But is no one responsible, no one answerable for these acts? Anxiety and depression we all acknowledge, even vague guilt feelings; but has no one committed any sins?[5]

*Sense of Sin*

Today, especially through the pervasive influence of humanistic psychologies, we have unconsciously accepted a very strong bias toward human nature that would rule out any negative view of ourselves. Saying, "I'm OK," seems to exonerate us from any deeper understanding of the underlying motives that cause us to be self-centered in both word and deed. We have lost St. Paul's sense of individual and corporate sin (see Rm 7:24) and have accepted a

Pelagian view of human nature that excludes any need of God's grace to offset our basic inclination towards selfishness. We preach the perfectibility of human nature and practice a rugged, self-sufficient individualism that leaves no room for God or sin. We are taught from early childhood that "winning is everything," without any concern for how our selfish tactics may adversely affect others. Little wonder that so many Catholics, as members of this society, have fallen away from frequent participation in a sacrament which holds us to be personally responsible for our acts and insists that we confess those things which we do that are wrong.

As Pope John Paul II pointed out in his Encyclical, *Veritatis Splendor* ("The Splendor of Truth," Oct. 5, 1993):

"According to some, it appears that one no longer need acknowledge the enduring absoluteness of any moral value. All around us we encounter contempt for human life after conception and before birth; the ongoing violation of basic rights of the person; the unjust destruction of goods minimally necessary for a human life. Indeed, something more serious has happened: man is no longer convinced that only in the truth can he find salvation. The saving power of truth is contested, and freedom alone, uprooted from any objectivity, is left to decide by itself what is good and what is evil" (No. 84).

"Once the idea of a universal truth about the good, knowable by human reason, is lost, inevitably the notion of conscience also changes. Conscience is no longer considered in its primordial reality as an act of a person's intelligence ..., a judgment about the right conduct to be chosen here and now. Instead, there is a tendency to grant to the individual conscience the prerogative of independently determining the criteria of good and evil and then acting accordingly" (No. 32).

[But] "conscience is not an infallible judge; it can make mistakes" (No. 62). We can be thankful, as Catholics, that the Holy Spirit has provided us with tangible assistance to help us from falling into error. "Christians have a great help for the formation of conscience in the Church and her magisterium . . . 'For the Catholic Church is, by the will of Christ, the teacher of truth'" (No. 64).

## To Sin Is to Miss the Mark

From new studies in Scripture, we see sin as more than a violation of God-given laws. In the Old Testament sin is seen as anything, regardless of the cause, that prevents us from "hitting the mark, the bull's-eye." In the Byzantine Liturgy, before receiving the Eucharist, both priest and people pray together for the forgiveness of all sin, deliberate and indeliberate. In this context, sin is seen as anything that prevents God from being God in our life. It is as much the brokenness of our ancestors that we have inherited as it is our own willfulness. It is the "sin of the world" that Paul speaks of as our sharing in the original sin of our foreparents.

## Legalistic Approach and Magical Tendencies

Most people today are looking for a more personal encounter with the Lord in the Sacrament of Reconciliation. They are turned off by an impersonal and legalistic catalogue of sins which they had learned in early childhood when they were incapable of distinguishing between personal, moral responsibility and external, objective acts presented to them by authority figures as being sinful. They remember the times when they may have confessed as a sin having missed Mass, even though they were seriously ill or traveling in an area where there was no opportunity to attend Mass, and they recognize that something is seriously amiss here.

Karl Rahner explains this as the result of a legalistic approach to the sacrament which was inherited from our early childhood without reference to any subjective, inner motivation and which

8

tends to look upon the reception of the sacrament as a kind of magical solution to our feelings of shame and guilt.

How often do not people confess something "just in case," so that God will not have anything "on us," and as if one had to or could insure oneself against him, as though God could debit one with something when we ourselves did not recognize any clear duty?[6]

When confession is treated in this manner, as an objective, mechanical ritual that brings about (mainly through the absolution given by the priest) an increase of grace in our souls and a higher place in heaven, then its deeper significance as a source of inner healing and true conversion of our entire life to God is lost.

## Unhealthy Elements

One of the areas addressed by the new Rite of Penance was that of the relationship between the priest-confessor and the penitent, often characterized in the past as cold and impersonal. Confessors are specifically encouraged by the new Rite to be warm and welcoming in their celebration of the sacrament.

The priest should welcome the penitent with fraternal charity and, if the occasion permits, address him with friendly words.[7]

Who can say how many penitents have been turned away from this sacrament because they did not find the loving mannerisms of Christ apparent in the priest who represented him? Too often a confessor might probe unnecessarily for details regarding a certain sin, causing extreme embarrassment to the penitent. This might be attributed in part to the fact that the clergy were taught that they were to judge the seriousness of the sins committed in order to dole out a satisfactory penance for them. Occasionally the confessor would have to ask that a sin from one's past life be confessed so that he could absolve the individual. This created a false sense of guilt and seemed to deny that the sin or sins of one's past were really forgiven by God. Little emphasis was placed on the communitarian sense of sin and of the need to help the penitent to deepen his or her spiritual life. And as a result, many fell away from frequenting the sacrament.

## A New Rite Not So New!

After the promulgation of the new Rite, it was hoped in ecclesiastical circles that more people would return to the sacrament. But we have seen in parishes around the world no such return. Perhaps this failure to stir Catholics to a more frequent reception of the Sacrament of Reconciliation can be summarized in two reasons.

(1) Pastorally, the clergy have not taken the time to adequately explain to their parishioners what the new Rite was proposing and then to put the new Rite into effect. But (2) the main reason is the failure, in the document, to present a catechetical and theological integration of the text with the basic theology of justification.[8]

The role of the priest, rather than that of Christ, continues to be central in the new Rite of Reconciliation. The new Rite places upon the absolving priest the role of reconciler in the three ways which it outlines for the celebration of the sacrament.

## These three ways or Rites are:

(1) individual and private confession: a dialogue between the penitent and the confessor who, in the name of the Church, absolves the sins of the penitent. Absolution is the key element of the sacrament;

(2) a communal penance service: this is really not much different from individual and private confession except that it is done in the context of a communal celebration, and little time, if any, is given to dialogue between the penitent and the confessor. Individual absolution remains central;

(3) a communal celebration with general absolution and penance given to all present. This is reserved to "emer-

gency" situations when private confession would be difficult or impossible. The obligation to go to confession later and seek absolution from all serious sins remains.[9]

## The Centrality of Private Absolution

In the new Rites there is a positive affirmation of communal services as the "preferred" manner in which we are to receive this sacrament, as Vatican II declared in its *Constitution on the Sacred Liturgy*:

> It is to be stressed that whenever rites, according to their specific nature, make provision for communal celebration involving the presence and active participation of the faithful, this way of celebrating them is to be preferred, as far as possible, to a celebration that is individual and quasi-private.[10]

At the same time, in all three Rites we see the insistence on the necessity of going privately to a confessor to receive absolution. The new Code of Canon Law confirms the centrality of private confession with absolution imposed by a legitimate minister.[11]

## Mortal and Venial Sins

Many Christians are confused as to how to discern between mortal and venial sins, and what needs absolution and what can be forgiven in other ways such as through the other sacraments, especially the Eucharist, almsgiving, and other corporal and spiritual works of mercy.

The teaching of the Church on this matter is pretty clear but not necessarily clearly understood. What may be judged by one confessor to be a mortal sin may not be so interpreted by another. An area of particular concern to me has always been the emphasis on gravity of matter in any and all thoughts, words or deeds against the sixth commandment. A false sense of guilt is easily engendered in those of delicate conscience. As far as thoughts are concerned it is important to see how a thought develops and at what juncture we finally wake up to what is being presented to our conscious awareness as an occasion to choose to live out our baptismal vows to renounce sin (the darkness of self-centeredness) and Satan, and to put on the values and mindset of Christ.

The Church states that for a sin to be mortal it must involve something truly serious, it must be given sufficient reflection, and it must be given the full consent of one's free will. "Mortal sin exists when a person knowingly and willingly, for whatever reason, chooses something gravely disordered" (*Veritatis Splendor*, No. 70).

Up to now in this matter, Western Christianity has been under the influence of St. Augustine, who used the Latin terms *lethalia* and *mortifera crimina* for mortal sins, and *venialia, levia* and *quotidiana* to refer to venial sins. In 1984, Pope John Paul II affirmed that the distinction between mortal and venial sins is not found in the Bible,[12] in spite of the teaching of many moralists who interpret the text of 1 Jn 5:17 as making a clear distinction between those sins which lead to death and those that do not.[13]

## A Blurring of Distinctions

What we see happening in the Church in this regard is a rapid breakdown in the minds of many Catholics of the almost supreme authority of the priest-confessor to determine what is objectively a "serious" sin and what is merely "venial." Influenced by social structures and cultural preconditioning, to say nothing of their own inherited dysfunctional family traits, penitents by and large are fashioning their own sense of sinfulness, generally unaided by the objective norms of the Church. Their more or less informed conscience is their only guide. The distinction between sin and inappropriate behavior begins to blur. People begin to look to psychoanalysis, sensitivity training, or group discussion to dispel feelings of guilt rather than to turn to the Sacrament of Reconciliation.

## Dawning of a New Awareness

We have seen some of the reasons why the majority of Catholics no longer receive the Sacrament of Reconciliation with any consistent regularity. From the loss of a sense of sin to the feeling that absolution is no longer relevant in our day and age, they have allowed the reception of the sacrament to fall into disuse. In spite of this general malaise, however, there are signs of a dawning of a new awareness of what the Holy Spirit is doing in the Church, East and West. We see it, in fact, in the two principal forms of the Sacrament of Reconciliation which have evolved: private and communal. It's not a matter, as Ladislaus Orsy, S.J., pointed out, "of the authentic versus the unauthentic, or the perfect versus the imperfect, but a struggle between two genuine, but limited expressions of Christian tradition."[14]

There is always a need for balance between the permanent core truths taught from apostolic times about repentance and reconciliation, and the many changes that have taken place down through the ages. These changes will continue to take place under the inspiration and guidance of the Holy Spirit. Such historical changes are external and visible, but they stem from inner movements received in the Church members through the guidance of the Holy Spirit. Thus we can study these new changes as authentic manifestations of God's merciful forgiveness mediated to us in our sinfulness.

We must begin, therefore, with a brief study of those historical forms and rituals which emerged as valid expressions of reconciliation which are rooted in the truths Christ revealed to his Church. Then, grounded both in the permanent and in the changeable, we can seek out various ways such permanent truths can be expressed today to make this sacrament, through the Holy Spirit, more the sign of our encounter and reconciliation as sinners with Jesus Christ, our sinless Savior.

Chapter Two

# HUMAN SINFULNESS,
# REPENTANCE AND CONVERSION

*The Gold of the Holy Spirit*

The many positive elements found throughout the historical evolution of the Sacrament of Reconciliation are like deposits of gold hidden here and there as a result of the operation of the Holy Spirit. To discover them, we must look beyond some of the accidental emphases which the different rituals and teachings in both Eastern and Western Christianity placed on aspects of sin and its forgiveness in the past. To do this, we must begin with the common reality of our human sinfulness and our need for conversion throughout our lives. We need to study the essential elements of repentance if we can even suggest the possibility of changes that will make the Sacrament of Reconciliation a better manifestation of God's merciful forgiveness mediated to us in our sinfulness.

The fullness of God's revelation on repentance and conversion is found in the primordial Sacrament of Reconciliation, Jesus Christ. But first, let us study how, even before the advent of Christianity, the Holy Spirit worked to reconcile individuals to God through various cultural rituals.

## *Restless Searchings of the Human Heart*

By studying some of the common elements found in the rituals and practices of non-Christian religions, we can understand more clearly what Jesus teaches us in the Sacrament of Reconciliation. He came, not to destroy, but to make perfect what the Holy Spirit had begun before the Word of God became flesh and dwelt among us. Let us keep in mind the words of the Fathers of Vatican Council II:

> Likewise, other religions to be found everywhere strive variously to answer the restless searchings of the human heart by proposing "ways," which consist of teachings, rules of life, and sacred ceremonies.
> The Catholic Church rejects nothing which is true and holy in these religions. She looks with sincere respect upon those ways of conduct and life, those rules and teachings which, though differing in many particulars from what she holds and sets forth, nevertheless often reflects a ray of that Truth which enlightens all men.[1]

People of every religion and culture feel a basic need to be reconciled with God after committing sins against their conscience or against the established taboos of society. They deal with this need through repentance and, in many groups, through some form of confession of their guilt and shame accompanied by an offering of expiation and sacrifice to the Supreme Being, their Creator.

Aware of this, we can more readily understand the teachings of Jesus Christ on human sinfulness, repentance, conversion and redemption, and be more ready to explore the practices and rituals of the Sacrament of Reconciliation in the early Church, practices and rituals which were in many ways simply the continuation and fulfillment of these earlier non-Christian rites as found especially in the Jewish religion.

Any suggestions we may propose to effect a vital rejuvenation of the Sacrament of Reconciliation must be grounded in the teachings and practices inspired by the Holy Spirit through the ages.

## Human Sinfulness

Dr. Karl Menninger defined sin in this way:

> Sin is a transgression of the law of God; disobedience to the divine will; moral failure. Sin is failure to realize in conduct and character the moral ideal, at least as fully as possible under existing circumstances; failure to do as one ought toward one's fellow man (Webster) . . . The wrongness of the sinful act lies not merely in its nonconformity, its departure from the accepted, appropriate way of behavior, but in an implicitly aggressive quality — a ruthlessness, a hurting, a breaking away from God and from the rest of humanity, a partial alienation, or act of rebellion.[2]

But human sinfulness far exceeds any mere rational definition. The true nature of sin consists in a human person's refusal to love God and neighbor unselfishly. It is slavery to the self-centeredness into which we are born. It is a movement away from communities of loving intimacy in a direction *inward, backward* and *deathward.*[3]

God created us to share an intimate friendship with him by making us according to his own image and likeness (Gn 1 and 2). But the biblical story of the fall of Adam and Eve shows us that some terrible, original calamity wrenched and destroyed the harmony in love that we were called by God to enjoy through our free cooperation with his grace.

Cardinal John Henry Newman wrote as follows of the certainty of original sin and the transmission of its effects to all created, earthly beings in a world that is "groaning in travail" as a result (Rm 8:22):

> If there be a God, since there is a God, the human race is implicated in some terrible aboriginal calamity. It is out of joint with the purpose of its Creator. This is a fact, a fact

17

as true as the fact of its existence; and thus the doctrine of what is theologically called original sin becomes to me almost as certain as that the world exists, and as the existence of God.[4]

## The Dynamics of Sin

The scriptural view of sin (original and personal) links our rejection of God's eternal plan with his indelible mercy in giving us a Messiah, a Redeemer, in his own Son, Jesus Christ. Sin has to do with the abominable abuse of our free will, manifested in our turning away from God's loving design for us (Ep 1:4). At the same time, as St. Paul (Ep 2:1-6) points out, it is intertwined with God's infinite mercy and forgiving love:

> And you used to be dead in the sins and transgressions by which you followed this world's way of life, obeying the ruler of the power of the air, the spirit that is currently at work in God's disobedient followers. We all once lived among them in the desires of the flesh; we did what the flesh and our imagination wanted and were, by nature, children of wrath, like the rest of them. But God is rich in mercy and because of the great love he had for us, even when we were dead in our transgressions, he brought us to life together with Christ — it is through grace that you have been saved — and raised us and has us sit together with Christ in the heavenly realms so that in the coming ages he could show the extraordinary riches of his grace in his kindness toward us in Christ Jesus.

## Sin and Repentance

If sin comes through the abuse of free will, repentance comes to us through its proper exercise. Refusal to love God and neighbor becomes cooperation with God's infinite mercy.

Sin imprisons us in a vicious cycle of defilement and hate;
Repentance frees us through purification and love.

Sin brings us punishment (self-inflicted) because it is a violation of the best in our God-given human nature;

Repentance erases that punishment because, by humbly claiming our personal guilt in turning from God and the community, it
restores our relationship with them both.

Sin wounds the innermost part of our psyche where the
presence of God abides;

Repentance heals that wound and makes us once again "sharers
in God's very own nature" (2 P 1:4).

Sin separates and alienates us from the triune life of God within
us;

Repentance removes the illusion of God's absence and makes
him even more present to us through humble conversion.

Sin promises pleasure and power which are fleeting and
illusory, followed by mourning, weeping and tears;

Repentance promises us weeping, mourning and tears, followed by everlasting joy which no one can take from us.


## The Ritual of Repentance

*Repentance* as a noun and *to repent* as a verb come from the Latin
word, *paenitere*, which means to be sorry, to grieve, to regret. As a
religious term it denotes in general a person's attitude, will and
behavior, usually accompanied by feelings of contrition and remorse for past transgressions and perhaps accompanied by some
form of restitution. It is to be found in many, but not all, religious
traditions.[5]

Repentance is usually expressed in a ritual designed to repair
a breach in one's relations with the gods and any individual or the
entire community. A central aim of religion is to promote good
relations with the gods. Any violation of the perceived will of the
gods (sin) ends such a relationship. Repentance, therefore, em-
braces all the religious rituals or means thought necessary to

restore that relationship, including the confession of sins, restitution, acts of purification and the offering of expiatory sacrifices, washing away all defilement and leading from sin to salvation.

## Confession

Frequently repentance is accompanied by some form of confession, the verbalization of wrongs committed, and the acceptance of blame for their personal and social consequences.[6] Such confession can be made directly and privately to the gods in a penitential prayer, or to a credentialed representative, or publicly before the community. The rituals that accompany the confession are designed as a catharsis in which remorse and sorrow are replaced by peace and joy. In many religions, penitents may wear sackcloth and ashes, cover themselves with mud, inflict pain on themselves, undergo a fast, or abstain from sexual relations. Restitution or compensation is also often an integral part of such penitential rites.

## Judaism

In Judaism we find a gradual development away from the rituals practiced by their neighbors and adapted by the Israelites to a more conscious and personalized sense of guilt accompanied by conversion and a return to the covenantal love of God.[7]

In Hebrew two words are used to describe the richness of the Jewish concept of repentance that would lay the groundwork for the rite of penance employed by the early Christians. *Shav* in Hebrew means to turn back. Repentance is a turning back to God, as Joel exhorts the Jews around 400 B.C.: "Come back to me with all your heart, fasting, weeping, mourning. Let your hearts be rent and not your garments, turn to Yahweh your God again, for he is all tenderness and compassion, slow to anger, rich in kindness, and ready to relent" (Jl 2:12-13).

The other more encompassing word for repentance in Hebrew

is *teshuvah* (in Greek, *metanoia*). The concept of *teshuvah* (change of heart, conversion) is very rich and is contained in the preaching of Jesus on repentance as the necessary condition to enter into the Kingdom of Heaven (Mk 1:15; Mt 3:2).

## Claiming One's Sinfulness

The prayers said on Yom Kippur, the great Jewish Day of Atonement,[8] were recited in the lifetime of Christ and are still recited in Jewish synagogues throughout the world. In them we find three essential elements of repentance: (1) The individual, within the unity of the Jewish community, seeks both a communal and an individual acquittal from sin through atonement. (2) Both the individual penitent and the mourning community seek together a catharsis, or purification, from the stains of sin. (3) The test of true repentance and the acquittal from sins committed is to be found in the ongoing process of conversion apparent in an individual's turning from sin and its occasions in the future.

Fundamental to the celebration of Yom Kippur is the gathering of the community to make a public acknowledgment of their sins. There can be no true repentance or conversion unless sins are acknowledged. In the Old Testament, Aaron offered a bull and a goat as a sacrifice for the sins of the people (Lv 16:6ff.). King David publicly acknowledged his sin and begged God's mercy, asking him to wipe away his faults, to wash him clean of any guilt, and to purify him from his sins (Ps 51:1-2). "I have my sin forever in my mind, having sinned against none other than you, having done what you regard as wrong" (Ps 51:3-4).

The mere acknowledgment of one's sins is not enough, however, unless such an act flows out of an inner, heartfelt sense of remorse and shame. God seeks from us not so much the sacrifice of animals as a broken and contrite heart, which he will never spurn (Ps 51:17). The inner personal sorrow that we have for our sins is linked to our sense of tremendous loss. God desires, as Isaiah testifies, "to comfort all those who mourn and to give them for ashes a garland, for their mourning robe the oil of gladness" (Is 61:3).

The Septuagint translation of the Old Testament uses the Greek word *penthos* 120 times to indicate the grief experienced by those in public or private mourning. Such compunction and sorrow bring to us, broken in spirit, a sense of tremendous loss. It is a sorrow at remembering our audacity in turning away from God, which in turn brings with it a feeling of dread at the prospect of cutting ourselves off from God forever and losing our eternal salvation.[9]

### Remembrance of Sins of the Past

For both Jews and Christians, true repentance is bound up with the concept of time. As God was ever mindful of us in the past, he never forgets us in the present, nor will he in the future. When we recall our past sins, we also remember how loving and faithful God has been to forgive them. This fills us with sorrow for our past transgressions but also fills us with hope and inspires us to confess them, promising to adhere more completely to God in the future.

Were it not for our hope that God's eternal mercy and love will help us to transform them, it would not be a healthy thing for us to dwell on our past sins. But in times of repentance we must revisit the past to discover who we have been and now are, so that in the future we can, with God's grace, grow beyond that in our love for God and neighbor. Putting God at the absolute center of all our future striving is at the very heart of true repentance and ongoing conversion.

### The Experience of Personal Sins

The more deeply we feel the effects of sin, the more apt we are to appreciate the humble goodness of God who died on the cross to free us from sin and its consequences. Even the slightest offense against God's love, which endures forever, should fill us with holy fear and a keen sense of how far we have to go to be worthy of the salvation which he won for us. This awareness is what inspired St. Francis of Assisi and all the great Christian saints to claim that they were the greatest of sinners and unworthy to be numbered among his followers.

Rabbi Joseph B. Soloveitchik in his classic book, *On Repentance*, describes the feeling of unworthiness caused by sin in this fashion:

> The sense of abomination intermingles with the sense of shame and opprobrium. The sin appears to the sinner like a terrible monster; he is filled with shame through having come into contact with the "bestial"; and out of the shame, the sense of abomination, of mourning, and of the other emotions which comprise the sense of sin, he begins to ascend the ladder of "Repentant Man," at last attaining repentance itself.[10]

### The Sanctity of the People of God

No one can be truly repentant of past sins without desiring firmly to live a life more dedicated to becoming holy as God is holy. Yet such holiness can only be attained by returning to the *Qahal*, the "Called Out People of God," the community of believers. In the Old Testament, God never calls an individual to come back to him without also inviting him or her to reenter the *Knesset Israel*, the House of Israel, the community of the chosen people.

The Jewish people found their uniqueness as individuals in their belief that God is and always has been faithful to the whole community of the House of Israel. When they sinned, they felt alone, cut off from the community and hence from the Creator, and unable by their own power to regain their union with him. It was God's *hesed* (covenant) based on his *emet* (undying fidelity to the community) that stirred in them the hope of an eventual return to his forgiving love. God's faithful love was available to them only by returning to the community to which God had pledged that love.

Know then that Yahweh your God is God indeed, the faithful God who is true to his covenant of mercy down to the thousandth generation towards those who love him and keep his commandments (Dt 7:9-10).

## Faith of the Patriarchs and Prophets

Sin breaks the covenant, cutting an individual off from God and the community. Repentance makes it possible for the penitent to return to both. Recalling the patriarchs and the prophets, the penitent publicly acknowledges his or her sins and renews the covenant by promising to love God once again "with all my heart, with all my soul, with all my mind, and with all my strength," and "to love my neighbor as myself." As an individual, the penitent cannot demand forgiveness of God, but as a member of the community, he or she can ask for this forgiveness with full confidence in a spirit of exultation and joy as the prayers recited even today on Yom Kippur so clearly show. The strength and power of this prayer to touch God lies, not in anything the individual penitent can say or do, but solely in God's faithful promises to forgive the sins of the House of Israel if the members demonstrate authentic repentance.[11]

## Two Ways

The future is built on the past foundations of God's faithful love and the reality of our past sins. Now, in the present moment in which we confess our need of God's forgiveness, we renew our commitment to follow God's covenant anew. And as we do, God speaks once again to us and holds out to us a future transformed by his undying love.

See, today, I set before you life and prosperity, death and disaster. If you obey the commandments of Yahweh your God that I enjoin on you today, if you love Yahweh your God and follow his ways, if you keep his commandments, his laws, his customs, you will live and increase, and Yahweh your God will bless you in the land which you are entering to make your own . . . I have set before you life or death, a blessing or a curse. Choose life, then, so that you and your descendants may live in the love of Yahweh your God, obeying his voice and clinging to him; for in this your life consists (Dt 30:15-20).

## *A New Enlightenment*

Repentance brings us out of the darkened world of sin and shadows into the fullness of God's light and unconditional love. Our past failings can become the stimulus for our greater adherence to God's holy will in all things, and for more humble service to our neighbors in the future. St. Augustine aptly describes this seeming paradox in this way:

> I am so sure of your love that I dare to come to you even with my unfaithfulness; You are able to love even my infidelity.[12]

No longer do we find ourselves running *away from* God. We run *to* him. God's promise is fulfilled in our present experience and we are filled with joy: "Happy are those who mourn; they shall be comforted" (Mt 5:5).

In our next chapter we will learn how Jesus is the primordial Sacrament of Reconciliation and the fulfillment of Israel's prayer for a Messiah who would bring salvation to the House of Israel. In the meantime, let me close with a fitting quote from Simone Weil (+ 1943), the Jewish mystic drawn to Christianity. It speaks of how our life is transformed in every way by the experience of God's forgiving love.

> We live in a world of unreality and dreams. To give up our imaginary position as the center, to renounce it, not only

intellectually but in the imaginative part of our soul, that means to awaken to what is real and eternal, to see the true light and hear the true silence. A transformation then takes place at the very roots of our sensibility, in our immediate reception of sense impressions and psychological impressions. It is a transformation analogous to that which takes place in the dusk of evening on a road, where we suddenly discern as a tree what we had first seen as a stooping man, where we suddenly recognize as a rustling of leaves what we thought at first was whispering voices. We see the same colors. We share the same sounds, but not in the same way.[13]

Chapter Three

# JESUS: THE LIVING SACRAMENT
# OF GOD'S MERCIFUL RECONCILIATION

## *Jesus, Living and Active*

Jesus is the primordial Sacrament of Reconciliation, as revealed in the New Testament and encountered through the teachings and sacraments of the Church. It is, therefore, to the Gospels that we must go to establish that Jesus is the Way and the Truth and the Life (Jn 14:6), our Divine Savior, the One who reconciles us to the Trinity.

## *Jesus, The Healing Light*

Jesus died on the cross to take away our sins. But the Good News is that, by his resurrectional presence through his Holy Spirit, he lives on in his Body, the Church. By his lifegiving power, we can be set free from our sins and reconciled to God whose divine life is given to us in Baptism.

Jesus risen is still a light that shines in the darkness of sin and death. This darkness inhabits all of us, and through us covers the entire world. This concept is beautifully portrayed in the midnight Easter service of the Byzantine rite churches. The priests and deacons along with the entire congregation march out of the church, leaving it in total darkness. The main celebrant, from outside the closed doors, knocks and then begins to sing with joyful triumph: "Christ is risen from the dead, trampling down death by death, and granting life to those in the tomb!" He and the congregation enter into the darkened church with lighted candles as they shout out the oft-repeated refrain: "Christ is risen! He is truly risen!" In such a celebration the experience of Jesus as the Light who is still among us in the Church community, divinizing us by pouring out upon us his loving Spirit who dispels all sin and darkness, is made extremely vivid and real.

## The Message of Reconciliation

Dr. Joachim Jeremias outlines four elements in the preaching of Jesus that offer people the possibility of entering into the Kingdom of God through personal and communal repentance.[1] These are: (1) the return of the quenched Spirit; (2) the overcoming of the rule of Satan; (3) the dawn of the reign of God; and (4) the Good News preached to the poor and accepted by them.

J.H. Charlesworth concurs that these are the four central themes found in the preaching of Jesus.[2] Jesus spoke to ordinary listeners in parables about the Kingdom of Heaven or the Kingdom of God as the goal of human striving. He presented the Kingdom as something which begins small like a mustard seed but grows and bears fruit, or like wheat sown in a field, or yeast mixed into dough, or a treasure hidden in a field. Other images he used were of the responses of people toward God's call: the wise and the foolish virgins, an obedient and a disobedient son, a king and his three stewards to whom he entrusted his money.

Jesus emphasized the role of repentance as a means of reconciliation with God and entrance into the Kingdom. This reconciliation would be ratified through an outpouring of the fullness of the Spirit which Jesus could not give until he himself was glorified (Jn 7:38-39). Satan's influence would be diminished by the penitent's

28

acceptance of the new life which Jesus, the God-man who was crucified for our sins, brings. The penitent's role is to respond to this gift of the Spirit by allowing it to bear fruit in his or her life through the love which they share with others.

## *The Poor Have the Gospel Preached to Them*

Jesus came as the mercy of the heavenly Father incarnate to bring all of God's children, created in his image and likeness (Gn 1:26-27) to share in the divine life of the Trinity. Jesus insisted that only those could receive the Kingdom of God who were born again, had the qualities of a child, and were poor in spirit like the *anawim* (Jn 3:3; Mk 10:15; Mt 5:3).

Jesus insisted that his listeners experience a conversion of heart, becoming small and humble in their own eyes, receptive to God's loving activity in their lives. Otherwise, they will not recognize the Kingdom of God present in their midst. A child, in his "littleness" and need, cries out to God on whom he depends for everything and thus becomes the model for those who wish to enter into the Kingdom. The poverty of spirit of which Jesus speaks is a spiritual poverty that recognizes one's nothingness before the absolute sovereignty of God.

In his turn, God has promised to comfort those who mourn, to show mercy to the merciful, to enable the pure of heart to see him, to call peacemakers his own children, and to give the Kingdom of Heaven to those who suffer persecution on his behalf. They are to rejoice and be glad, for a great reward will be given them (Mt 5:6-12; Lk 6:21-23).

## *Metanoia*

Jesus preached a turning away from one's self-absorption by turning totally to God. This conversion, *metanoia* in Greek, is a gift that God gives to those who unselfishly seek to return to him as their true

Center. It does not consist in the performance of certain rituals in order to merit such a reward. It is primarily a matter of the heart, a turning within so as to effect an inner revolution of sorts whereby we put on the mind and values of Jesus (Ep 4:17ff.).

To enter the Kingdom of God one must be born from above, not only by water but by the Holy Spirit (Jn 3:3, 5). This requires a "losing" of one's life, a turning completely away from self to surrender completely to God as the inner, directing force of one's life. The seed must die to itself if it is to bring forth new life a hundredfold (Jn 12:24-25). It is oftentimes a slow process in which God only gradually becomes the axis around which our lives revolve. It involves the enlightenment of the Holy Spirit who reveals to us the meaninglessness of worldly, self-centered values and the joy inherent in surrendering to God's holy will in all things.

## Jesus Speaks of God's Forgiving Mercy

How can we come to know God's reconciling, compassionate love for us except through his Word made flesh? St. John (3:16) assures us that God loves us so much that he gave us his only begotten Son so that whoever believes in him will not die, but live forever. He will be healed, made whole and reconciled to the Father.

Faith, hope and love are infused into us by the Spirit sent by the risen Lord. In them, we can accept the revelation of Jesus' historical life on earth as recorded in the New Testament and explained by his Church. We do not have to conjure up ideas of what God might be truly like. We *know* what God is like through our faith in the historical person of Jesus of Nazareth, true God and true man, of one substance with the Father. We believe the Good News that, for love of us, he freely became one of us to restore us to friendship with the Father.

In the Incarnation, God's Word "pitched his tent" among us by becoming totally human while remaining fully divine by nature. This is why he was able to say: "To have seen me is to have seen the

Father" (Jn 14:9). He is the Way, the Truth and the Life (Jn 14:6) who leads us to the unseen God (Col 1:15).

## *Jesus Speaks of God's Forgiving Love*

By the power of the Holy Spirit, we can believe that this historical person, Jesus of Nazareth, born of a woman (Gal 4:5), is the exact image of the heavenly Father in whom the fullness of loving mercy dwells. His teachings about reconciliation give us a new outlook on life. By turning prayerfully to his teachings on mercy, forgiveness and reconciliation, especially in his parables, we ground our faith in the truth of God's living Word, who is Truth itself incarnate.

God's mercy and burning desire to reconcile us in our sinfulness to him are revealed in the teachings of Jesus in the Gospels. Contemplating him in the Gospels brings us to an ever-increasing awareness of his resurrectional presence, living in us individually and within his Mystical Body, the Church. Allowing him to unveil God's mercy and reconciliation to us in the context of our present human situation, we find it easy to commit ourselves in obedience to him. This abiding in the compassionate and forgiving love of the risen Lord has the power to gradually transform us into compassionate and forgiving persons ourselves.

## *Jesus Teaches Mercy and Reconciliation*

Jesus is God's living Word, sent to communicate to us all we need to know about God, our human destiny, and the purpose of creation. He is more than a prophet who has been anointed and given a mandate to speak on behalf of God. Jesus *is* God's Word incarnate; he *is* the message. He is the living Word of God who cannot deceive nor be deceived.

If we obey his words, we will be divinized: "If anyone loves me, he will keep my word, and my Father will love him, and we shall come to him and make our home in him. Those who do not love me

31

do not keep my words. And my word is not my own: it is the word of the One who sent me" (Jn 14:23-24).

## Jesus Spoke in Parables

Jesus' teachings about mercy and reconciliation are predominantly presented in the synoptic Gospels of Mark, Matthew and Luke in the form of parables which, as a literary form, have their roots in Old Testament and rabbinic literature. In his beautifully simple stories, Jesus unfolds for us the sublime truth of his Father's forgiving mercy and reconciliation, and of how great God's love is for us whom he created in his own image and likeness. Whether he is describing himself or teaching us about his Father's loving mercy toward us, what applies to Jesus, the Word incarnate, applies also to the Father. (See John Paul II, *Dives in Misericordia*, "On the Mercy of God," Nov. 30, 1980, Footnote 5, p. 51.)

God is a Good Shepherd in the person of Jesus Christ. He leaves the ninety-nine righteous sheep and searches out the one who gets lost. He joyfully carries it on his shoulders and, on returning home, calls his friends to celebrate with joy the finding of his lost lamb (Lk 15:4-7).

As a woman with ten drachmas searches out one she may have lost, God searches out with great diligence the person who may have gone astray. As she rejoices with her friends at having found her lost coin, so God rejoices in retrieving a lost sinner: "In the same way, I tell you, there is rejoicing among the angels of God over one repentant sinner" (Lk 15:8-10).

## The Prodigal Father

St. Luke's Gospel has been called the Gospel of God's Mercy, especially in its series of parables which highlight the infinite, compassionate mercy of God toward us. Undoubtedly the best-known story in the Bible and the favorite of many is that of the heavenly Father's reconciling love and mercy as told in the parable about the prodigal son.[3] It is a dramatic presentation told by Jesus to a group of tax collectors and sinners to illustrate the compassionate concern of God for the sinner. The drama has three actors. The father represents God, the heavenly Father. The younger son, the second actor in the drama, leaves home after demanding all of his inheritance. Having squandered it all on "riotous living," he finds himself relegated to the humiliating task of feeding some farmer's swine. It is at this point that he begins to reflect on the direction his life has taken and experiences a real conversion or change of heart. He gets up and starts for home, hoping to be allowed to work on his father's land as one of the hired hands. On the way, he thought of what he would say to his loving father. He was determined to ask his forgiveness and to make amends for having offended him. The third actor in the drama, the elder son, has diligently served his father all his life, but is resentful when the father forgives his brother and takes him back. He lacks the love he ought to have and his father has to reprimand him (Lk 15:11-32).

*A Rejoicing Father Who Forgives Sinners*

Scripture exegetes stress the setting in which Jesus delivered this parable. He was responding to the Scribes and Pharisees who were asking his disciples why their Master welcomed tax collectors and sinners and even ate with them. He wanted to teach them that his fellowship with sinners is an image of how the heavenly Father goes out to the broken ones of this earth and offers them his forgiveness and reconciling love. At the same time, he wanted to encourage all "tax collectors and sinners" to continue coming to him and to rely on God's great mercy.

It is hard for us to understand what a tremendous statement Jesus was making about his heavenly Father in relating this parable. In Jewish families, the father of the family was almost an autocrat, ruling with dispassionate power. Jesus must have shocked his listeners as he told them of their heavenly Father who waited with great anguish and patience for the return of his ungrateful, younger son and who showed equal loving concern for the self-righteous older boy.

He sets the scene for the reconciliation, indicating that the father, while the son was still afar off, caught sight of him coming down the road. Forgetting his hurt pride and patriarchal dignity, the father joyfully runs out to greet his returning, repentant son, throwing his arms around his neck and kissing him affectionately (Lk 15:20).

The first truth that Jesus wishes to reveal to us in this parable is that, sinners though we are, we can impact the very life of God. We see how the father sadly waits for the return of his sinful son, and then runs out to embrace him in joyful reconciliation when he does come back. This is Good News. God, our heavenly Father, truly rejoices as he shows us mercy in our repentance.[4] His heart leaps with joy and all the angels in heaven join in the celebration when one of God's children repents and returns to the Father's embrace.

The second truth is that the Father of Jesus is a waiting, merciful, forgiving, loving God. His is like the love of a mother, full of affection, ready to suffer and weep for her children. Jesus imaged such a Father when he wept over Jerusalem (Lk 19:41). "How often I longed to gather your children, as a hen gathers her brood under her wings, and you refused!" (Lk 13:34; Mt 23:37; *Dives in Misericordia*, #5).

## A Waiting God

Both the Old and New Testaments show that God is a God of pathos. God in his essence is immutable and perfect. But the triune God freely chooses to burst forth through his uncreated energies of love to be the intimate Ground of all creatures' being.[5] God is transcendent and absolute subsistence in himself, yet, through his free will, he has chosen to be supremely relative to his created world. He did not have to create us and the material world. Yet he freely does so and sees it to be very good (Gn 1:31). He, therefore, freely wills to give and receive love from us, his human children.

As the father in this parable respects the freedom of his sons, so God respects our freedom and does not coerce us. He offers his self-gift to "entice," or to "allure" us to return his gift of love.

## *Jesus Acts as Reconciler of the Father*

Jesus' first believers saw in him a man filled with the compassion of a mother for her suffering children, the protective love of a shepherd for his sheep, the total self-giving of a bridegroom for his bride as he healed the multitude of sick persons brought to him everywhere he went. "He went round the whole of Galilee teaching in their synagogues, proclaiming the Good News of the Kingdom and curing all kinds of diseases and sickness among the people" (Mt 4:23-24; Mt 10:1).

How great was his compassion when he raised the dead son of the widow of Nain and returned him to his sorrowing mother! (Lk 7:11-17). He had mercy on the woman who had suffered from an issue of blood for twelve years, and immediately healed her (Lk 8:40-48). He raised Jairus' daughter from the dead out of mercy toward her grieving parents (Lk 8:40-56), and cured the centurion's servant at a distance because he admired the faith of this Roman officer (Lk 7:1-10).

To the sinful woman who anointed him while he dined at the home of Simon the Pharisee (Lk 7:40), Jesus likewise showed compassion and forgave her sins "because she loved much," which is the essence of true repentance. He manifested God's love and compassion when he healed the Gerasene demoniac (Lk 8:26-39) and when he cured the epileptic boy at the petition of the youngster's father (Lk 9:37-43). In doing so he showed that he had power over Satan and the kingdom of darkness. Not even the Sabbath law of rest could prevent his bringing the healing balm of the Father's love to those who were suffering (Lk 13:10-17). "The Sabbath was made for man," and not vice versa (Mk 2:27). And with a touching bit of humor, he summoned Zacchaeus down from his perch in the sycamore tree to bring forgiveness and reconciliation to him and to his household (Lk 19:1-10).

## Fullness of Mercy and Reconciliation on the Cross

The greatest revelation of God's forgiving love is presented to our eyes as we stand prayerfully at the foot of the cross and contemplate Jesus' compassionate and loving concern: for his mother and the disciple whom he loved: "Mother, behold your son; son, behold your mother" (Jn 19:25-27); for the sinner who shared a similar fate: "This day you shall be with me in paradise" (Lk 23:43); and for those who were responsible for his crucifixion: "Father, forgive them, for they do not know what they are doing" (Lk 23:34).

The terrifying agony, the extreme sense of utter abandonment, the darkness that engulfed his spirit are indelibly etched on our minds and hearts as we contemplate the suffering of Jesus on the cross in those final moments before his death. We cannot even begin to imagine what it cost God in the passion and death of his Son to manifest his infinite mercy toward us. Such an intuition is reserved to the *anawim*, the poor in spirit, the little ones in God's Kingdom who are not scandalized by the cross and God's self-emptying love: "For God's foolishness is wiser than human wisdom, and his weakness is stronger than human strength" (1 Cor 1:25). Jesus is the human image of the invisible God, the concrete expression of the reconciling, merciful love of the Trinity toward us.

## Death and Resurrection

If we are to be true to God's revelation in the New Testament, we can never separate the death of Jesus from his resurrection. Theologians up to the 20th century generally overemphasized Jesus' death on the cross as the fitting sacrifice to atone for our sins and to ransom us from eternal damnation. They almost totally neglected the mystery of the resurrection of Jesus as the fulfillment of his earthly life, of his teachings and suffering and death.[6]

We read in the *Baltimore Catechism* in answer to the question of what our redemption means:

> By the redemption is meant that Jesus Christ, as the redeemer of the whole human race, offered his suffering and death to God as a fitting sacrifice in satisfaction for the sins of men, and regained for them the right to be children of God and heirs of heaven.[7]

This view of our redemption made our salvation seem to be a past event that happened in the historical moment when Jesus died on Calvary. His death was not intrinsically connected with the glorious triumph of his resurrection. Such a view tended to distance us from a living encounter with the Redeemer as the risen Lord.

F.X. Durwell, C.SS.R., in his classic treatment of the resurrection, intrinsically ties the death of Jesus on the cross to our encounter with the risen Lord in Scripture, in the sacraments, and in the guidance of the Magisterium. He writes:

> But Christ is not fixed in death as in a state following an act; the sacrifice remains actual. Not in the act of happening, of course, but in its final point, the moment of consummation. Indeed, as Scripture describes it, Christ's glorification can be defined as a permanent act beyond which Christ's existence never passes. Our Lord's redemptive death is also ordered towards the glory in which it is fulfilled, and with which it coincides, as in any change the end of one way of being coincides with the beginning of another. In the ever-actual permanence of his glorification, Christ's death itself thus remains eternal in its actuality, fixed at its final point, as the moment of its perfection.[8]

## The Glory of the Cross, Our Reconciling Hope

God brought Jesus back from the dead "to become the great Shepherd of the sheep by the blood that sealed an eternal covenant" (Heb 13:20). In his various covenants, God pledged to be faithful to his promise to protect and share his life with his chosen people. This reaches its culmination in the resurrection of Jesus, who fulfills all other covenants as, by the outpouring of his blood, he establishes a New Covenant: "This cup is the new covenant in my blood which will be poured out for you" (Lk 22:20).

Jesus suffered and died for love of his followers and went forward into a completely new existence which he now makes possible for his disciples to share: "I am he who lives. I was dead but now I live forever and ever, and I hold the keys of death and the underworld" (Rv 1:18). St. Paul puts it this way: "Jesus was handed over for our offenses and was raised to restore us to fellowship with God" (Rm 4:25), he "died and was raised to life" (2 Cor 5:15) in order that we might have eternal life.

The resurrection is not only pivotal to the life and mission of Jesus, it is fundamental to God's actions throughout all human history. That is why Paul insisted: "If Christ has not been raised, then you are still in your sins" (1 Cor 15:17).

## Paradoxes in Christianity

Over and over again in the New Testament we find antitheses and paradoxes which seek by various metaphors and symbols to express the mystery of our sharing in the very life of God himself as a result of his own initiative. In his preaching, Jesus often linked death and life, darkness and light, bondage and freedom. Above all he lived these contradictions. He was the light who came into the darkness, even though the darkness did not comprehend him (Jn 1:9-11). He came to bring life, and that more abundantly, to those who were sick and dying (Jn 10:10). He was the power by whom and in whom and for whom all things were created (Jn 1:2; Col 1:16), yet he appeared in weakness as an infant in Bethlehem, and was crucified in humiliation on the cross in Jerusalem. It was when he was lifted up and emptied himself on the cross that he was exalted in glory by his heavenly Father (Ph 1:10). He descended into our world, was tempted in all things but never sinned (Heb 4:15) in order that we might ascend with him into heavenly glory (Ep 4:8-10). His seeming defeat by the powers of evil led to his eternal victory over sin and death. His shame was turned to glory. And he holds out to us the same opportunity to suffer with him in order to reign with him in glory (Rm 8:17).

Jesus is the second Adam who offset the fall of the first Adam. Through the Church — his Body which extends his living, risen presence into our time and space — he makes it possible for us to put off the old self and to put on the new person in him (Ep 4:22; 2 Cor 5:18). His resurrectional life is present in us through the Holy Spirit who divinizes us and makes us "spiritual" persons (Rm 8:9-11) who no longer live a perishable and corruptible life but the incorruptible life of God.

Jesus has destroyed sin and death and has restored us to fellowship with the heavenly Father (Rm 8:16; Gal 4:6). We have been baptized into his death, and he has raised us to new life as children of God and heirs of heaven. Though no longer physically on this earth, through his Spirit he remains always with us in his Mystical Body, the Church.

## Christ's Church: Another Sacrament of Reconciliation

Jesus, as we have said, is the primordial Sacrament of Reconciliation. As he did while he was living on this earth, he continues to justify and to reconcile to the heavenly Father all who come to him in true repentance. And he does so through his Mystical Body, the Church, another sacrament of reconciliation: "Those he called he also justified, and those he justified he also glorified" (Rm 8:30). In another place, Paul goes so far as to say: "Even when we were dead in our sins, he brought us to life together with Christ — you have been saved by grace — and raised us and had us sit together with Christ in the heavenly realms" (Ep 2:6). Jesus shares his resurrectional life with us through his indwelling presence.

Yet we know from our own sad experience and that of the Church as a whole that we can still sin. We live in a state of tension between the glorious light of Christ and the all-pervading darkness of sin.

### Shared Authority

Jesus is the Head of the Church. As such he has imparted power to forgive sins to his Church's pastors. He is always the principle of that forgiveness, the one who imparts new life, provides nourishment and sustenance so that we, as his members, can be built up into an edifice of praise to God: "Joined together and united by all the supporting ligaments, when each part is working as it should, (Christ) the head causes the body to grow and build itself up in love" (Ep 4:16).

The Church is where the family of God comes together in brokenness and love. In it all human beings are invited to enter into God's *kairos*, the graced moment of his healing and reconciling care. The Church becomes a sacrament of reconciliation when it abides in love and shares that love with others (cf. 1 Jn 4:12).

In the next chapter, we will examine various rituals and doctrinal expressions of reconciliation, and see how they may develop in the future. Before doing this, however, we need to show how Christ has endowed his Body, the Church, through his immediate disciples, with the charism to teach the truths of God with authority. This charism is exercised under the mandate of the risen Lord, and will continue under the guidance of the Holy Spirit until the end of time.

## *Jesus Risen Is Still Present Through Shared Authority*

Jesus is present to his members through the graces and charisms he gives: "Grace has been given to each of us according to the extent of Christ's gift" (Ep 4:7). It is the work of the hierarchy of the Church, through loving service, to bring these charisms together in harmony and order to build up the Body of Christ. Jesus first gave the charism of authority to Peter (Mt 16:19), and then to the other apostles (Mt 18:18; Jn 20:22-23). This special authority given to the apostles and their successors, the consecrated bishops of the Church, allows them to exercise the priestly, prophetic and royal authority of Christ, from whom they have received it and in whose name and according to whose mind they are to exercise it.[9]

## *Tradition and Traditions*

In our study, we must always keep in mind the distinction between Tradition (the permanent truths which Christ taught, lived by and handed down to his apostles) and traditions (the historical accretions promulgated by Church authorities in imperfect, but sincere attempts to express that Tradition). This important distinction has been highlighted in the *Constitution on Divine Revelation* of Vatican II:

> This tradition which comes from the apostles develops in the Church with the help of the Holy Spirit. For there is a growth in the understanding of the realities and the words which have been handed down. This happens through the contemplation and study made by believers who treasure these things in their hearts (cf. Lk 2:19, 51), through the intimate understanding of spiritual things they experience, and through the preaching of those who have received through episcopal succession the sure gift of truth. For, as the centuries succeed one another, the Church constantly moves forward toward

the fullness of divine truth until the words of God reach their complete fulfillment in her.[10]

The Church, unlike any other existing human institution or organization, is a living organism. A human person develops from infancy through childhood to adolescence and then adulthood, yet there is a permanent core of "personhood" and uniqueness that persists through these changes. So it is with the Church, the Body of Christ, infused with the Holy Spirit.

The Gospels are the written memories of the first apostles who passed on the Tradition, the core of Jesus' words and deeds. Jesus commanded them to be faithful to all he had taught and done: "Go therefore and make disciples of all nations . . . teaching them to observe all that I have commanded you" (Mt 28:19-20).

Jesus is God's inexhaustible revelation and truth. To him, living as the risen Lord in his Body, the Church, his members must be faithful until the end of time. But he also taught his disciples: "But when he comes — the Spirit of truth — he will lead you to the whole truth" (Jn 16:13).

As Ladislaus Orsy notes in regard to the history of the Sacrament of Reconciliation, historical evolution cannot be considered as a movement away from an earlier imperfect development to a later more perfect one. Orsy concludes:

The reason is that, at one time or another, each system had the support of the universal Church, certainly of the universal episcopate. The opposing views were not about the permanent core of the sacrament, but about its temporary historical expression — even if the bishops did not quite realize it. The conflict, therefore, must not be explained as the fight of the authentic versus the unauthentic, nor as the fight of the perfect against the imperfect, but as a struggle between two genuine, but limited, expressions of Christian tradition.[11]

## Conclusion

Jesus Christ did not leave his disciples a detailed ritual that he meant to be adhered to as the only sacramental expression of the joyful reconciliation of the heavenly Father with his repentant children.

Let us now turn to the history of the Sacrament of Reconciliation to see how the Holy Spirit in the Church inspired various ways of presenting, doctrinally and ritually, the Father's call to his children to receive his reconciling love as manifested by the risen Jesus and his Holy Spirit. Only by understanding this can we come, humbly and respectfully, to formulate new external expressions that perhaps will help us to better receive in repentance God's reconciling love.

Chapter Four

# THE SACRAMENT OF RECONCILIATION IN THE APOSTOLIC AND PATRISTIC CHURCHES

*The Evolution of a Sacrament*

Most Catholics and Orthodox who frequent the Sacrament of Reconciliation today have an anachronistic view that this sacrament has always remained ritually in a form very similar to what we have been familiar. To show how in reality this sacrament has evolved over the years, let us embark on a journey, starting with the origins of this sacrament as found in the New Testament, post-apostolic and patristic writings.[1]

The historical development of the Sacrament of Reconciliation is best understood in the organic growth process found in a seed. The acorn in some potential way already contains the full oak tree in embryonic form. As the acorn develops, something substantially enduring is always present even though radical and externally obvious changes take place in the growth process.

In a similar way, the New Testament attests to the fact that Jesus Christ forgave sinners and passed this power on to his immediate followers, the apostles and their successors. This is the "seed" that would evolve over centuries into various ritual expressions and doctrinal emphases discovered in the long history of the Sacrament of Reconciliation.

*Jesus Ministered God's Reconciliation*

Jesus went out in compassion and mercy to the broken and the maimed, the publicans and the prostitutes, the poor and the marginalized ones of this earth to bring them to an inner purity of heart by reconciling them to his Father.[2]

His disciples personally witnessed Jesus in his ministry of reconciliation. They themselves personally experienced his forgiveness of their own sins, especially their betrayal of him in his passion and death. But, above all, by the outpouring of his Holy Spirit after his death and resurrection, they were convinced that Jesus wished to share with them his power of forgiving sinners. He commissioned them to go forth to all nations, baptizing them in the name of the Trinity. "Whose sins you shall forgive," he told them, "they are forgiven them" (Jn 20:23).

St. Peter on Pentecost shows how seriously the apostles of Jesus carried out his mandate. When some of the Jewish crowd heard Peter witness to the death and resurrection of Jesus and asked what they must do to receive what the disciples had received, he replied: "You must repent and be baptized, every one of you, in the name of Jesus Christ for the forgiveness of your sins" (Ac 2:38).[3]

*Shared Power in Forgiving Sins*

By sharing his power to forgive sins with his disciples, Jesus made it something tangible and concrete on a social level through the mediation of the bishops and priests of the Church. In Matthew's Gospel we see Jesus sharing this power first with Peter and then with the other disciples:

I will give you the keys to the Kingdom of heaven. Whatever you bind on earth shall be bound in heaven; and whatever you loose on earth shall be loosed in heaven. (Mt 16:19)
Amen, I say to you, whatever you bind on earth

shall be bound in heaven, and whatever you loose on earth shall be loosed in heaven. (Mt 18:18)

In John's Gospel we find the last of the three classical New Testament texts that have traditionally been used throughout the centuries to illustrate that Jesus bestowed upon his apostles the power to forgive sins:

> Receive the Holy Spirit. Whose sins you forgive are forgiven them, and whose sins you retain they are retained. (Jn 20:22-23)

Contemporary Protestant and Catholic commentators caution us not to read too much into these texts, especially not to restrict their meaning solely and exclusively to a power given only to Peter (Mt 16:19) or to all the apostles (Mt 18:18 and Jn 20:22-23).[4] Raymond Brown summarizes his finding in regard to the text from John (20:22-23), which we can also aptly apply to the texts from Matthew, and this should suffice for our purposes:

> In summary, we doubt that there is sufficient evidence to confine the power of forgiving and holding sin in John 20:22-23 to a specific exercise of power in the Christian community, whether that be admission to Baptism or forgiveness in Penance. These are but partial manifestations of a much larger power, namely, the power to isolate, repel, and negate evil and sin, a power given to Jesus in his mission by the Father and given in turn by Jesus through the Spirit to those whom he commissions.[5]

In the apostolic Christian communities, we do not find a uniform penitential rite, but we do see an awareness (from these three classical texts and many others) that the apostles and their immediate successors knew that the Church had been given the mission to continue the ministry of reconciliation of sinners to the Father.[6]

## The Church Community as Sacrament of Reconciliation

It would be erroneous to apply these cited texts exclusively to a power Jesus gave Peter and the other apostles which they were to exercise over the other members of the Church. The Christian community, the Church, made up of all fervent members, was the locus or place of reconciliation. Throughout Chapter 18 of Matthew's Gospel we see that the entire Christian community is called to bring about reconciliation.

Thus we see traces of the earliest penitential practices within the Church. The entire apostolic community was aware of the possibility of sin and of forgiveness for its members. Such small communities were made up of new adult converts who underwent a stringent spiritual and doctrinal catechesis. Through Baptism all their previous sins were remitted. In communal prayer, but above all, in the celebration of the Eucharist and in the performance of good works toward those in need, they were strengthened so as not to fall into serious sin.

Another way of refraining from serious sin and division within the Church-community was the custom of fraternal correction as Jesus taught in Matthew 18:15-17:

> If your brother sins against you, go and tell him his fault between you and him alone. If he listens to you, you have won over your brother. If he does not listen, take one or two others along with you, so that every fact may be established on the testimony of two or three witnesses. If he refuses to listen to them, tell the church. If he refuses to listen even to the church, then treat him as you would a Gentile or a tax collector.

Other examples of mutual correction, the prayer of the community, and a form of confession of sins to fellow-Christians, are

48

found in Mt 18:19-20; Gal 6:1-2; Jm 5:16-20; and 1 Jn 5:16. Thus we conclude that the power given to Peter and the other apostles is not an absolute power, but is intimately united to the entire Christian community. The exercise of this power over sin by Peter and the apostles and succeeding bishops is always an act of Christ's forgiving mercy, which reconciles sinners to God in the Mystical Body of Christ, the Church. Both the community and its leaders are related in the exercise of this reconciliation.[8]

## *The Separation and Correction of Grave Sinners*

Sin after Baptism was not expected in the Church among the fervent early Christians. Yet sin was an existential reality which forced an exercise of the power to bind and loose sins given to the Church by Christ. J.A. Favazza considers this tension that has always existed in Christ's Church as a struggle between leniency and rigorism. "Attempts to deal with this reality were not a matter of following predetermined rituals or patterns of behavior but of balancing the mission to forgive 'not seventy times but seventy times seven times' (Mt 18:22) with the call of Jesus to 'be perfect, as your heavenly Father is perfect'" (Mt 5:48).[9]

What was the Church to do, for instance, in the case of a Christian committing a serious sin that was a great scandal to the community and to non-Christians wishing to enter the Church? The New Testament does not give us any uniform penitential procedure to deal with post-baptismal sinners. Ways of handling this problem only gradually developed out of the rabbinic discipline of "banning" and from the practices of such groups as the Essenes.

## *The Power of Excommunication*

Paul gives us a clear example of the apostolic practice in regarding to "banning" one who was a scandal to the Christian community. This is the case with the incestuous Corinthian who was living as husband to his own step-mother (1 Cor 5:1-13). Paul writes:

49

A man who does a thing like that ought to have been expelled from the community. I, for my part, although absent in body but present in spirit, have already, as if present, pronounced judgment in the name of Jesus, on the one who has committed this deed: when you have gathered together and I am with you in spirit with the power of the Lord Jesus, you are to deliver this man to Satan for the destruction of his flesh, so that his spirit may be saved on the day of the Lord. (1 Cor 5:2-5)[10]

Paul, the leader of the community, and the community itself, isolate themselves from the sinner. This is done out of charity, first for the sake of the healthy members of the community, and secondly that the sinner may come to his senses and be restored to the community through repentance and amendment. If the sinner is cut off from the community, especially from participating in the Eucharist, this is a temporary isolation sought only to encourage the sinner to repent and be restored to the Church.

Paul insists that those guilty of "impurities, fornication and debauchery" (2 Cor 12:21; 13:1-2) do penance and be set aright in their relationship to God and the Christian community. Interior repentance was necessary for any reconciliation. In Hebrews 6:4-8, the impossibility of repentance for apostates stems, not so much from any apostolic custom of refusing them absolution, but rather from the inflexibility of their own moral dispositions which kept them from admitting any wrongdoing and seeking forgiveness.

Another text from Hebrews (12:16-17) warns Christians against tolerating those who are impure or irreligious in their midst, stressing that God will not pardon those who remain unrepentant.

## Confession of Sins

When John the Baptist baptized in the river Jordan, the sinners "confessed their sins." They were following a Jewish practice for divine forgiveness, especially on Yom Kippur (Mk 1:5; Mt 3:6). In

Acts 19:18, we read that many of those in Ephesus who had become believers "came forward and openly acknowledged their former practices." The same expression is used by the apostle John (1 Jn 1:9) to indicate that confession of one's sins is a vital part of being reconciled to God and the Christian community. "Then he who is faithful and just will forgive our sins and cleanse us from every wrongdoing."

James, too, indicates the practice of sincerely acknowledging one's sins by some form of confession when he ends his directives to the presbyters or priests, saying: "If he has committed any sins, he will be forgiven. Therefore, confess your sins to one another and pray for one another, that you may be healed" (Jm 5:15-16).

Here we see a practice stressed in the apostolic writings such as the *Didache* and the *Letter of Barnabas* that would indicate some ritual among the healthy members of the community as they met to celebrate the Eucharist. The *Didache* (c. 100-120 A.D.) describes a communal confession of sin when the early Christians gathered for the Eucharist:

> In the assembly, you will confess your sins and not come to prayer with a bad conscience (4, 14).
>
> And on the day of the Lord, assemble for the breaking of the bread and the Eucharist, after having first confessed your sins, so that your sacrifice may be pure (14, 1).[11]

### Submission to Leaders of the Church

Before the end of the 1st century we find documents testifying to the practice of reconciling any sinner, no matter how grave the sin, provided there were true repentance and a confession of the sin either to the bishop or his delegate, a presbyter or priest. We will see in the 3rd century a radical change in thinking that swung from mercy to a strict rigorism. This new rigorism allowed for only one post-baptismal reconciliation and for serious penances lasting for long periods of time, with continued social repercussions lasting until death. Once enrolled by the bishop in the "order of penitents," the person would always be considered a penitent, even after having received formal reconciliation from the bishop and the community.

The Epistle of Pope Saint Clement to the Corinthian Christians (c. 96 A.D.) illustrates his intervention as peacemaker toward leaders of a schism in that church. He writes:

Therefore, you who set up the faction, submit yourselves to the presbyters, and be disciplined to the penitence. Bowing the knees of your heart, learn to be in subjection, putting away the assertive and overweening arrogance of your tongue; for it is better for you to be found small and of no account in the flock of Christ, than while seeming to have eminence to be torn away from his hope.[12]

This quote certainly shows the awareness in the 1st-century Church of the power of the presbyters to reconcile those in schism. It may also have reference to a special ritual, but this is not certain.[13]

St. Ignatius, bishop and martyr of Antioch (+ c. 115 A.D.), stressed the necessity of union with the bishop and that those in schism may be brought to unity through repentance and submission to the bishop: "In all, therefore, who render penitence the Lord accords remission if they undergo penitence unto the unity of God and the council of the bishop."[14]

St. Polycarp of Smyrna (c. 135 A.D.), in keeping with the attitude of the early Church in Asia Minor, so influenced by the spirit of John the Evangelist, counsels priests to be "just and impartial to all, bringing back the wandering, having an oversight of all the weak, not neglecting the widow or the orphan or the poor . . . not quickly according belief against any, not relentless in judgment, knowing that we all are debtors in sin."[15]

Thus we can say that the Church from the beginning until about the middle of the 2nd century believed that any sin, no matter how grave, could be forgiven if the sinner was truly repentant. We see the plea to bishops and priests to be full of compassion and merciful to sinners once it was established that they were truly repentant. The granting of pardon and the imposition of an "adequate" penance were left up to the individual bishop. In some cases, unfortunately, leniency led to laxity, with the sinners becoming confirmed in their sin.

## *The Shepherd of Hermas*

Hermas, a layman of the Church of Rome, wrote the *Shepherd* circa 150 A.D. Around the time that he wrote, many Christians had apostatized under persecution. The question arose as to how to deal with sinners who had so violated their baptismal promises. Hermas promoted a rigorist policy that would endure until the 6th century.[16]

Almost obsessed by his conviction that the end of the world was imminent, Hermas called sinners to seize the final chance for forgiveness. His central teaching on penance is found in his "fourth mandate" in a colloquy between Hermas and the angel of penance:

> I have heard, sir, said I, from certain teachers that there is no other repentance than that one when we went down into the water and received remission of our former sins. He said to me, you have heard correctly, for so it is. He who has received remission of sin ought never to sin again, but to live in purity . . . For those who have already believed or are about to believe have no repentance of sins, but have remission of their former sins. For them that were called before these days, the Lord appointed repentance, for the Lord knows the heart . . . The Lord therefore, being full of compassion, had mercy on his creation and established this repentance. But I tell you, said he, after that great and solemn calling, if a man should be tempted by the devil and sin, he has *one*

repentance. But if he sin repeatedly, it is unprofitable for such a man, for hardly shall he live.[17]

Johannes Quasten summarizes the important elements in Hermas' teaching on penance very well:

1. There is a saving repentance after Baptism. This was taught, as we have seen, by the New Testament and the early Church writers before 150 A.D. What is new in Hermas' doctrine is that there is *only one* opportunity to be forgiven for sins committed after Baptism.
2. No repentant sinner is excluded, regardless of the gravity or nature of the sin involved.
3. Due to Hermas' expectation of the imminent end of the world, he insists that penance must be prompt and must produce an amendment of life, otherwise the sinner risks incurring eternal damnation. There can be no sinning and repentance after confessing one's serious sins.
4. The sinner must enter into a complete *metanoia*, a complete conversion, and reform his or her life. This is manifested in the willingness to make atonement by voluntary chastisement and fasting, and by praying for the pardon of the sins committed.
5. Such justification from sin through penance is not only a purification, but also a positive sanctification.
6. The Church is intrinsically necessary for salvation. The good Christians along with the bishop and presbyters are to pray for the sinner. What the formal rite of reconciliation was to be is not developed.[18]

### Elements of a Penitential Rite Appear

Next to St. Augustine, Tertullian had the greatest impact on theology in the early Western Church. He was born in Carthage about 155 A.D. and converted in Rome to Christianity. He returned to Carthage, probably as a priest, and there wrote profusely, leaving a lasting influence on Christian theology. About 207 A.D. he left the Catholic Church and became a member of a rigorist sect known as Montanism.

Tertullian made three major contributions to the theological development of the Sacrament of Reconciliation:

1. In his treatise *On Repentance* (*De Paenitentia*),[19] he insists with Hermas that there is a second penance, a "plank" of salvation thrown to the drowning sinner which God in his mercy "has set up in the vestibule to open the door to such as knock, but only once, because this is already the second time" (Ch. 7).
2. After Tertullian's embrace of Montanism, he wrote his treatise *On Modesty* (*De Pudicitia*), where he denies any power of the keys to the ecclesiastical hierarchy to bind or loose. He rejects his earlier Catholic position by introduc- ing the distinction between sins that are remissible (lighter, venial sins) and others that are irremissible. The Church has no power, he insists, to forgive such great sins after Baptism, and even the intercession of the martyrs for the guilty cannot avail.[20]
3. Of all the early Christian writers through the 3rd century, Tertullian gives us the most detailed picture of the primi- tive Christian penitential procedures. However, he does not offer us a complete service of how a sinner is enrolled into the "order of penitents" or how, after performing the assigned penance, that person is returned by the bishop or presbyter to full membership in the eucharistic commu- nity.

He gives us some details about *exomologesis*, literally, "the confessing of sins," to the bishop or assigned priest "as to Christ himself." This was to be done privately in order not to defame the penitent or expose him or her to the civil courts in case of civil crime. Tertullian tells us that part of the *exomologesis* included confession, and mentions other details of physical penances and prayers to be said.

From his treatise *On Repentance*, we see that, entering into the "order of penitents," the sinner is for some assigned time excluded from participating in the Eucharist with other members.[21] The sinner joins other penitents in the vestibule and is not allowed to enter into the main body of the church where the Eucharist is celebrated. He gives a rather graphic description of how a penitent conducts him or herself in undergoing the confession of sins (*exomologesis*):

> Exomologesis, then, is a discipline which leads a person to prostrate and humble himself. It prescribes a way of life, which, even in the matter of food and clothing, appeals to pity. It bids him to lie in sackcloths and ashes, to cover his body with filthy rags, to plunge his soul into sorrow, to exchange sin for suffering. Moreover, it demands that you know only such food and drink as is plain; this means it is taken for the sake of your soul, not your belly. It requires that you habitually nourish prayer by fasting, that you sigh and weep and groan day and night to the Lord your God, that you prostrate yourself at the feet of the priests and kneel before the beloved of God, making all the brethren commissioned ambassadors of your prayer for pardon.[22]

The Church had always made a distinction between venial and grave sins. It was the latter sins that required a sinner to do public penance for a required number of years, the penance being determined by the local bishop. Tertullian, on becoming a Montanist, excluded all grave sins as irremissible, contrary to the Catholic teaching that all serious sins were remissible after repentance and due penance.

## Apostasy and Martyrdom

The persecution under Decius (250 A.D.) occasioned many martyrs, but also many weaker Christians who apostatized. As soon as the danger was over, many of the apostates sought reconciliation and restoration to the Church, relying often on "letters of peace" given by martyrs about to be executed for the faith. St. Cyprian claimed that "thousands of certificates were daily being given to those who sought them."[23]

The great difficulty, not only with the problem of reconciling the apostates, but also with which sins required serious penance, came from inconsistent norms determined by the local bishops. Some laid down extremely rigorous conditions, while others were more lenient. Thus a uniform policy was of utmost urgency. Letters were exchanged between Cyprian and other leaders in Carthage and the Pope. Cyprian insisted that long and difficult penances should be maintained until the end of religious persecutions, when a Council could be held.[24]

Thus the Councils of Ancyra (314), Neo-Caesarea (314-323), Nicaea (325), Laodicea (c. 344-363) in the East, and the many African, Spanish, and Frankish synods in the West produced their own laws. Popes Siricius, Innocent I, Leo I, Felix II, Hormisdas, and Gregory the Great added their decisions in papal decretals. Many penitential statutes were brought together by certain bishops and writers to form the *Apostolic Constitutions* and the *Apostolic Canons*. These were taken largely from the *Didascalia* (c. 500), consisting mostly of canons from the African Church, especially of Carthage.

Writings and penitential letters of Peter of Alexandria, Basil, Gregory of Nyssa, and John Chrysostom in the East, and those of Ambrose, Pacian of Barcelona, and Augustine in the West added to the material that gradually jelled into law and acquired canonical status. Longer penances and various levels of penance which one must move through before the community were multiplied.

St. Gregory the Wonder-worker, bishop of Neo-Caesarea in Pontus (c. 233-270), witnesses to five degrees of penitents modelled on the pattern of admitting catechumens to Baptism. These were: the mourners, the hearing ones, the fallers, the bystanders and those who finally were able to participate with the other Christians in the Eucharist.[25]

Other severe conditions discouraged sinners to manifest themselves in the "order of penitents" and made the Sacrament of Reconciliation an act that was postponed until the death-bed. Once a penitent, one was considered always to be penitent, as one had still after reconciliation to submit to severe restrictions, ecclesiastically and socially. Former penitents who underwent the public confession of their sins could not become a priest, serve in the army, attend public spectacles or marry. If already married, they had to give up conjugal intercourse.

By the 5th century onwards, practically no one entered into such a rigorous discipline in order to be reconciled. Several Church Fathers from the 5th century complain that grave sinners were receiving the Eucharist without entering the "order of penitents." Some bishops as Caesarius of Arles counseled younger persons and married couples to put off such rigorous penance until old age. Also we find that clergy who had publicly sinned were not subject to such *exomologesis* or public confession, thus making the sacrament not one of universal application to all sinners.[26]

*Gradual Reform*

Reform was brought about gradually, both in the West and the East. In the West, the Celtic penitential practice began to influence ordinary Christians to want a more personalized and private form of confession to a priest, even for lesser sins out of piety and devotion. The Eastern Churches followed their own course toward the decline of excessive rigorism and the almost total neglect of public canonical penance.

St. John Chrysostom rebelled against rigorism and the teaching that the three capital sins — apostasy, homicide and adultery — could be forgiven only once after Baptism. In his voluminous writings, Chrysostom rejected the graded system of penance and insisted that the value of penance had to be judged by the inner dispositions of the penitent. For the ordinary good Christian there were other ways of receiving God's reconciliation, such as confession, contrition, humility, almsgiving, prayer, and the forgiveness of others.[27] With Chrysostom, no capital sin lies outside the present mercy of the Lord, and no limit is assigned to how often a sinner might be reconciled.

One cause of a lessening of rigorism in the Eastern Churches corresponded to the influence of the Celtic monks in the West, that is the powerful influence of monasticism in the East. In the East, confession to monks was stressed, especially by the bishops who came out of their ranks. There was even confession to those monks who were not ordained priests, if they were holy and skilled as physicians of souls, expert in the ascetical and mystical life.

In their capacity of confessors, the monks veered away from the canonical aspects of the Sacrament of Reconciliation and the long duration of penances. They stressed the infinite mercy of God toward sinners and each penitent's inner dispositions of *penthos* or inner compunction. Thus by the 8th century in the East, public penances had been replaced with private ones. What was always extended to the dying in the West, even in the times of greatest rigorism, was developed in the East with the greatest flexibility and leniency through private forms of reconciliation for the ordinary Christians as well as for the more grave sinners.

It is now time to see the radical change in regard to the private rite of Reconciliation that developed from the 7th century down to our own days, both in the East and in the West.

Chapter Five

# DEVELOPMENT OF PRIVATE CONFESSION

*The Mediterranean Form of Reconciliation*

In this chapter, we will see how a new form of the Sacrament of Reconciliation began with the Celtic Churches. Their use of private confession would eventually greatly influence the Western Roman Church from the 5th century down to the present time.

Ladislaus Orsy indicates the two distinct points of departure that constituted different accents in rituals in the mode of receiving this sacrament.[1] The Mediterranean form of Reconciliation was based on a strong consciousness of the unity of the entire Christian community. Reconciliation was public, and was granted by the bishop after the penitent completed rather severe public penances.

The Mediterranean form of canonical, public repentance became excessively rigoristic, especially since penitents often suffered a permanent stigma, as mentioned in the previous chapter. Usually if a sinner relapsed into sin after repentance, no second chance for reconciliation could be had until death. These forms of public reconciliation were not suited for the young, and many ordinary people were repelled by them. The otherwise "good" Christians could, of course, receive reconciliation through the eucharistic liturgy or praying personally for pardon or performing fasts and almsgiving. But if they wanted to receive the Sacrament of

Reconciliation, this was the only way open to them, at least up until the 5th century.

Thus, this Mediterranean rite of public Reconciliation diminished to almost non-existence. The result was that the Churches had no universal ritual easily available to all Christians in their sinfulness to receive signs of God's forgiveness.

## Development of the Celtic Form of Reconciliation

The Celtic missionary monks and bishops first brought the popular use of private confession to the ordinary people who had had no adequate rite other than the Eucharist to provide for them the "place" to acknowledge their brokenness and need for a continued conversion.

The Celtic Churches of Ireland, Scotland and Wales (with England gradually becoming influence by the Celtic usages, especially in regard to the Sacrament of Reconciliation) developed largely during the 5th to the 7th centuries. These Churches at this time manifested a pronounced freedom from the domination of Rome, especially in matters of canon law, which even amounted at times to overt resistance as Kathleen Hughes describes:

> Celtic churches of the sixth and early seventh century recognized the popes as leaders of the Church and successors of Peter, yet they did not give up their powers of independent judgment. The British refused to accept Augustine of Canterbury, appointed by Gregory the Great, and Columbanus did not hesitate to argue and rebuke the popes.[2]

## A Monastic Church

In the 6th century an unusual phenomenon developed that made the Celtic Churches into monastic ones. The ecclesiastical center no longer was Armagh, but the monastery at Iona. Abbots and abbesses became more important than bishops. This was due in large part to the fact that these Celtic countries, especially Ireland, were predominantly rural with villages built around the dominating monastic center.[3]

Here, as in the Christian East, monasticism would, through its accent on spiritual direction, develop what would eventually become the private penance ritual which we associate with the Sacrament of Reconciliation. To understand this new development of private confession, we need to understand how monasticism evolved.

## Spiritual Direction in the Desert

Celtic monasticism was more influenced by the Egyptian and Syrian desert hermits than by Benedictine monasticism. The Celtic Churches picked up the Eastern Christian concept of the necessity of a spiritual director, a holy man or woman skilled in the deeper reaches of prayer and asceticism.

True inner silence led to the inner integration of one's entire being, of all the appetites of body and soul which were then put under the dominance of God. This interior determination to live only for God was carried out by sobriety and a constant vigilance (*nepis*) over one's thoughts. Much of Eastern Christian spiritual writing concerned itself with the psychology of thoughts: how to control the "passionate" thoughts and how to move into a "thoughtful" consciousness of the indwelling Trinity.[4]

It was, therefore, unthinkable both for Celtic and Eastern monks for an individual to advance in the spiritual life without a spiritual director.[5] Such direction was given by daily manifesting to the guide one's conscience, with all one's thoughts, inner movements and moods. This direction was a work of great Christian love of a master toward a disciple, but concretely of great discernment of the movements of the Spirit in the individual's life.[6]

This compassionate approach accentuated the mercy and love of the triune God. It was in direct opposition to the public, canonical rite of Reconciliation with its threats of excommunication and social stigma attached to those who freely declared themselves sinners. The accent was not on severe expiation for sins, but rather on a healing, personal encounter of the disciple with Jesus facilitated through the example and loving presence of the "elder."

### Eastern Churches and Monastic Influences

The Eastern, like the Western, Churches fell victim to the extreme rigorism of the canonical form of confession. Similarly, Eastern Christians, especially the pious laity, turned to the monks for spiritual direction. This movement away from rigorism can be seen in Patriarch Nestorius' abolition in the 5th century of the office of the priest-penitentiary (a priest-expert delegated to hear confessions and impose severe penances after the Decian persecution).

In the absence of any official supervision and control over sinners, people sought advice from monks on how to form one's conscience.[7] Such spiritual directors often mitigated the duration of penances assigned for serious sins. They stressed the inner healing of the soul through such practices as fasting, vigils, detachment from possessions, and so forth. By the 8th century, public penances were almost totally replaced by private ones.[8]

The juridical aspect lessened in the Eastern Churches, and reconciliation took on aspects of healing therapy. Monks, both ordained and not, abbesses and other spirit-filled women, became spiritual directors and reconcilers in a manner that was not canonical. Clearly such "confessions" would not fit the definition of the Sacrament of Penance as given in the Council of Trent (1551-1552), yet the practice continued in the East well after the 12th century.[9]

### Celtic Form of Reconciliation

By the beginning of the 6th century, a ritual structure for private, auricular confession appeared in the European countries evangelized by the bishops and monks of the Celtic Churches. Penitents in private confessed their sins to a priest and manifested proper repentance. They then received absolution and later fulfilled an assigned penance.

As in the East, such penances were drawn initially from the practices of the monks. But gradually, with so many people receiving this new form of Penance and with the low level of theological formation among the priests, there developed the so-called "penitential books." Written usually in Latin or Gaelic, they listed in detail various sins and indicated the appropriate penance to be assigned for them. This came to be called the tariff penance. The earliest Irish penitential book still extant was written in the mid-6th century by St. Finnian, abbot of Clonard (+ 549). It brings together the penitential customs of his time and greatly influenced the *Penitential* of St. Columban, which had enormous impact throughout Europe.

These penitential books became the principal way in which the Celtic rite of Reconciliation spread so very rapidly. There were two main missionary expansions in Europe. The first was initiated by St. Columbanus in the latter part of the 6th and into the 7th century. The second occurred in the last part of the 7th and first half of the 8th century. Willebrord, Boniface and other Celtic and Anglo-Saxon monk-missionaries used this private form of Penance, that could be repeated as often as a penitent felt the need to do so, to convert and reconvert Europe.

## Commutation of Penances

The Celtic and Germanic form of private confession became highly influenced by the secular laws which were eventually carried over into the administration of this sacrament.[10] The civil courts provided precise punishments for public crimes. These were also listed in the penitential books, called a tariff of penances. This was unfortunately similar to the canonical penances of the ancient "order of penitents." Only after the penance was completed would the penitent be reconciled to the Church. This was symbolized by receiving Holy Communion again, but without any ceremony involving the bishop and the community as in earlier times.

This seemed to negate the influence on the Celtic missionaries of the desert monks who always presented to the penitent a welcoming, merciful, personal encounter with the living God in the Sacrament of Reconciliation. The tariffs of penances were a throwback to the legalism of earlier centuries and tended to prolong the length and severity of the penances incurred by the penitent. The Desert Fathers never pretended to measure the severity of a penance by the type of sin committed.[11]

In Frankish civil law we find the *compositio*, which was the substitution of money payment for any required punishment. This was introduced into the Celtic form of private confession and adequate satisfaction for sins committed. Thus, a penitent could perform a required penance by substituting one form of penance for another, such as almsgiving, reciting numerous prayers, donating a specific sum for the upkeep of the parish church, or even hiring another to do the required fasting.

This civil law not only affected the ritual of the Sacrament of Reconciliation, but also impacted the medieval theological understanding of the death of Jesus as "vicarious substitution," the idea that Jesus took our place on the cross and accepted death as a punishment for our sins. This is developed in St. Anselm's theory of atonement and is to be found in the writings of many theologians who followed his lead.

### Penance, a Catechetical Tool

The Celtic form of private confession before a priest became a tremendous tool to catechize many. Under the Germanic invasions throughout northern Europe in the Dark Ages, whole groups of people were uprooted and merged with other groups. Various forms of folk-superstitions and customs began to blend. Even though the common people had become nominally Christian through mass baptisms enforced by the local rulers, they were hardly able to form their own Christian consciences.

The Celtic and Germanic missionaries used the penitential rite of private, frequent confession to create in the consciences of the ordinary people a Christian ethic. Such frequenting of the Sacrament of Reconciliation brought a renewal of self-worth, a healing of the habits of sin, and hope for improvement in the spiritual lives of such Christians.

## Disadvantages of the Celtic Form of Confession

In one way, such frequent confession among simple, ordinary Christians tended to trivialize the rite. The faithful often repeated the same list of venial sins or agonizingly dwelt upon their past offenses. What was lacking in such a ritual was fundamentally a sound theology of sin and reconciliation. Only since Vatican Council II have modern theologians begun to address the question of the regulations introduced into the Sacrament of Reconciliation by the Celtic form.

With the concept of the *compositio* or substitution of money for penances, there entered the idea of *indulgences*. These were works done, such as making pilgrimages to certain holy shrines, going on retreat, saying certain prayers, attending Mass at a "privileged" altar, that would equivalently compensate for other assigned penances. Such practices could easily distract the masses of Christians away from any true repentance, as they focused on the doing of good works to pay back or satisfy for the assigned punishment, rather than on a conversion of heart and an amendment of one's life.

## Good Friday Rites

An interesting ceremony, in no way universally used, was practiced in the 7th century in the Mozarabic Rite of Toledo.[12] This is called the Rite of "Indulgentia" as it appears in the Mozarabic Breviary, and it was made obligatory in the 4th Council of Toledo in 633 A.D. It was no doubt rooted in the Jewish services of Yom Kippur, the Day of Expiation. Communal as well as individual sorrow for sin was engendered through long and emotionally powerful pleading for forgiveness and reconciliation before an awesome but merciful God.

Some remnants of this rite can be seen in the present-day Roman Rite Good Friday services. In Toledo on Good Friday in the 7th century, the faithful would gather in their churches as penitents, regardless of whether they had sinned grievously or otherwise. During the service the faithful would stand to hear the plaintive prayers. Then all would kneel as the word, "Indulgentia" was chanted, and rise again after a period during which they would remain in silent and penitent prayer.

This was a quasi-sacramental penitential rite performed annually on Good Friday, without the private confession of sins or the imposition of a penance to be satisfied before receiving the Eucharist on Easter. No distinction was made between mortal and venial sinners, but the prayers seem to indicate that satisfaction for past sins committed had been made during the forty days of fasting and almsgiving during Lent.

## Tensions and Clashes Between the Two Forms of Reconciliation

Between 600 and 1000 A.D., the Sacrament of Reconciliation was celebrated in many different ways. A common thread that ran through all of them, however, was the belief that Jesus still reconciled penitent Christians through the power given to his disciples who passed it on to their successors, the bishops, and through them to the ordained priests. Yet many differences existed as to whom, by whom, in what ritualized fashion and how often pardon should be given.

The Celtic form of Reconciliation moved into the vacuum left by the Mediterranean form that, by the 6th century, had been effectively reduced to a rite received only on one's death-bed. Gradually as these two forms met each other in their individual strengths and weaknesses, tensions grew and chaos of a sort ensued.

Most of the tensions sprang from the position of the Frankish bishops. They were not against private confession, but saw the danger which the ever-spreading use of the penitential or tariff books brought to this sacrament. They were concerned with the question of Church authority in reconciling repentant sinners. These bishops wanted to control the imposition of penances and require a public ritual of Reconciliation. They feared that too many grievous sinners were receiving absolution of their sins without doing adequate penance for them.

These bishops saw the need for greater episcopal supervision to see that satisfaction was indeed made before absolution was given by the priest. Some of them sought to make a more authoritative compilation of official "canons" governing the penances to be imposed for various mortal sins. However, this only produced more penitential books with disputed authority.[13]

## Reforms of the Fourth Lateran Council (1215)

The Western bishops, especially in Spain and the Frankish Kingdom, did not surrender at once to the ever-popular Celtic form of Reconciliation. The Council of Toledo (589), reacting against the frequent confessions of the Celtic form, decreed that a Christian could receive absolution only once in a lifetime. We have seen, however, that in practice this discipline was increasingly ineffective.

The Synod of Chalon-sur-Saone in 813 denounced the penitential books because of the reputed errors they contained and the anonymity of their authors: "The errors are certain, but the authors uncertain" (can. 38).[14] The Synod of Paris ordered that the penitential books be burned.[15] The battles against these books and the practice of frequent private confession continued, but unsuccessfully.

Finally, the Fourth Lateran Council of 1215 formally accepted the Celtic form as the official way to receive the Sacrament of

Reconciliation. At a time when Catholics did not receive the Eucharist frequently, this ecumenical council decreed the following:

Let everyone of the faithful of either sex, after reaching the age of discretion, faithfully confess in secret to his own priest all his sins, at least once a year, and diligently strive to fulfill the penance imposed on him, receiving reverently, at least during Paschal time, the sacrament of the Eucharist, unless perchance on the advice of his own priest he judges that he should abstain for a time from its reception; otherwise, while living let him be denied entrance in church and when dead let him be deprived of Christian burial.[16]

It was later explained that this canon only applied to those who had committed serious sins.

### Importance of Priestly Absolution

By the 13th century, the Celtic form of Reconciliation had eclipsed the canonical Mediterranean form of public penance. Along with the influence of the Celtic missionaries to Europe, the Sacrament of Reconciliation was affected by the Carolingian reformation starting at the Court of Charlemagne. This reform stressed the central role of the ordained clergy in dispensing the sacraments.

Confession to holy lay persons, that is to the non-ordained, is found up to the Council of Trent in the 16th century. However, it is in the late Middle Ages that we see the administration of Reconciliation reserved exclusively to the priest.[17] In the 12th and 13th centuries, we see the beginning of high scholastic theology through the efforts of Peter Abelard, Peter Lombard, Peter of Poitiers, Alexander of Hales, and especially of Thomas Aquinas.

These theologians sought to describe the seven sacraments according to the causalities of Aristotle based on *matter* and *form*. They tried to dissect the essential parts of each sacrament and to show their relation to one another. "What is essential to forgiveness and reconciliation in this sacrament?" they asked. The main elements of the Sacrament of Reconciliation were: contrition, confession of sins, absolution, and satisfaction. "What is the role and importance of the priest?" With satisfaction made after the absolution given by the priest, they stressed that only he had the power of the keys to forgive all sins in the name of the Lord.[18] Under the influence of Anselm and his theory of atonement, theologians began to present the power of forgiveness as resting exclusively in the hands of the priest. Any satisfaction came to be regarded as a measure of punishment, a form of retributive suffering in order to balance the scales of justice.

## *The Formula of Absolution*

With the priests as confessors holding the sole power to forgive sins in the name of Christ, a shift appeared in the forms of giving absolution. Formerly absolution was a prayer that both the priest or bishop along with the community offered to God in the plea that God would grant pardon and remission of the penitent's sins.

This was followed by a statement declaring that the individual was absolved from further penances and penalties. Now this *declarative* formula of absolution from penances and penalties comes sharply into focus as the priest becomes central to the act itself of pardoning sins. "Whose sins *you* shall forgive, they are forgiven them" (Jn 20:23) was the Scripture cited for this emphasis. Even to this day, the form of the Sacrament of Reconciliation consists in these words of absolution pronounced by the priest: "*Ego* te absolvo" ("*I* absolve you"). No longer is there the *impetrative* formula of priest and penitent praying that God forgive the sins, dependent on the sorrow and repentance of the sinner.

In the Eastern Churches, the older Rituals (*Euchologia*), both Greek and Slavic, offer many forms of absolution, but all were *deprecative* or *impetrative* and were considered sufficient for a valid remission of sins if there was sincere repentance. This was true also for the formulae of the Latin Church before the 11th century.

### The Effects of the Council of Trent on Confession

With the convocation of the Council of Trent in the middle of the 16th century, we see the Roman Catholic Church bring to the doctrine and practice regarding the Sacrament of Reconciliation a definite shape and uniformity that has not fundamentally changed down to our present time.

In the canons of Trent, the necessity and institution of the Sacrament of Penance are stressed against the Protestant reformers.[18] It is declared a special sacrament, but not of the same rank of importance as Baptism and the Eucharist.

Trent defined that three acts required of the penitent are the "matter" of the sacrament: contrition, confession of sins and satisfaction. These acts were not to be viewed in a Pelagian way as meriting grace and forgiveness, however. The Council continually stressed in dealing with Penance that God alone in Jesus Christ is the sole efficient cause of our justification. Contrition and its accompanying acts of confession of sins and satisfaction for sins committed are seen as preparatory to receiving God's completely gratuitous forgiveness.

Canon 6 of the Council of Trent reads:

> If anyone shall deny that sacramental confession was instituted by divine law or is necessary for salvation; or shall say that the manner of confessing secretly to a priest alone, which the Catholic Church has always observed from the beginning and still observes, is at variance with the institution and command of Christ and is a human contrivance, let him be anathema.

The fathers of Trent had in mind the Protestants, who denied that Penance was a true sacrament. In reaction to them, they defended the form of the Sacrament of Reconciliation as it had been practiced for the last few centuries. We must keep in mind what P. Adnes writes, that it is a divine mandate for all to confess their sinfulness. But private confession to a priest is one of many modalities established by Church authorities and practices, conditioned by circumstances of time and place.[19]

## The Confession of Venial Sins

Canon 7 of Trent deals primarily with the confession of mortal sins as the primary purpose of the Sacrament of Penance. Yet it declares also that venial sins can be confessed as well. This does not mean that Christians are obliged to come to this sacrament exclusively to be pardoned of venial sins, however.[20]

Karl Rahner wrote a beautiful "apologia" for the frequent confession of devotion. He points out from the Council of Trent that there are many other ways to encounter the forgiving mercy of the Father toward us in our brokenness, especially in our "daily" sins that are not grievous. But for informed Christians to frequently approach the sacrament out of devotion to confess their venial sins can be most meaningful. Such an act is always a humble acknowledgment "that ultimately our sins are remitted by God's act alone and that ultimately he, the free God of grace, can be found only in his historical revelation, in his visible Church and his visible sacraments."[21]

## From Trent to Vatican II

From the 16th century to Vatican II, all Catholic theology and practice regarding the Sacrament of Reconciliation have been shaped by the teachings of Trent. We have briefly pointed out some of the positive elements that Trent asserted against the Protestant reformers who denied any special Sacrament of Penance and any absolving power given by Christ through the hierarchy to priests.

But one of the main weaknesses that still surrounds this sacrament came out of Trent's treatment first of justification, followed later by its treatment of the Sacrament of Penance. For both of these — penance and justification — the pastoral and the theological aspects must be interrelated, for one without the other doesn't work well. In this regard, Trent was less than fully successful.[22]

Jansenism which followed Trent in the early 17th century also affected the reception of the sacrament by exaggerating the gravity of all, even the slightest violations of the law of God or of the Church, emphasizing the unworthiness of all fallen human beings to approach the sacraments and the almost inevitability of severe punishment for sins.[23] Fear, not love, was the motivating force in the life of an observant Jansenist. And the mercy of God had little if any role to play in the Sacrament of Reconciliation.

So, as we can see, for the past 400 years in regard to the Sacrament of Reconciliation, there has been something of a divide between the theological, scriptural, and dogmatic perception of sin and a more pastoral, moral, and existential understanding. Since Trent, sin has been explained from a fundamentally canonical standpoint with little reference to its rightful theological and moral base grounded in Scripture. This has resulted in a legalistic approach to the sacrament and is one of many reasons why so many Catholics today do not receive it frequently. Somehow the head and the heart have to find common ground here so that the penitent's experience of encountering Jesus in the Sacrament of Reconciliation is something very personal, an encounter with some One who is not so much judge as friend, lover and Lord.

Let us now consider the new period which has been ushered in by the Second Vatican Council with its mandate for a renewal of the rite of Reconciliation, and with the three forms which were promulgated in 1973.

Chapter Six

# NEW RITES FOR RECEIVING
# THE SACRAMENT OF RECONCILIATION

*The Emergence of New Rituals*

The preceding chapters bear witness to a wide variety of forms of administering the Sacrament of Reconciliation down through history. This should not surprise us. Nor should we be surprised at other eventual changes in the way it is administered. We should rather expect, that because the Church and its members are constantly renewing themselves, new forms will emerge in the future. Such rites, under the guidance of the Holy Spirit, will hopefully bring Christians into an ever more personal experience of God's forgiving love and mercy.

The risen Christ lives as Head of his Church. His saving presence and power in the world is mediated through his Mystical Body which is historically situated in time and space. It is the work of the Church, the base Sacrament of Reconciliation, to manifest his love and mercy present to the world in and through his Body. Under the power of the Holy Spirit, the sacraments bring God's gift of salvation to the world.

The new rites promulgated on December 2, 1973 by the Congregation for Divine Worship allow us to discern how the Holy Spirit is operative today in the Sacrament of Reconciliation. By reflecting on these rites we hope to be able to humbly offer some suggestions aimed at an even greater renewal and appreciation of this sacrament for the future.

## Vatican II Mandates

Pope Gregory XVI in 1832 denied that there was any need to reform the post-Tridentine Church.[1] Indeed, in the centuries following the Council of Trent, the Roman Catholic Church saw very few official changes in regard to the sacraments, including the Sacrament of Reconciliation, either pastorally or theologically.[2]

Still as Kenan Osborne points out, there were situations that did alter the way both the theology and the practice of this sacrament were understood. The counter-reformation period brought about a gradual separation between dogmatic and moral theology. As a result, "in the long run the sacrament of penance was practically and on many occasions theologically explained through juridical and moral categories, rather than through biblical and theological ones."[3]

More positively, at the end of the 19th century and up to the middle of the 20th, scholars undertook historical research into the roots of the modern form of administering the sacrament. This research prompted a reform of the Tridentine form of Penance. The Second Vatican Council mandated such a change in these words: "The rite and formulas for the Sacrament of Penance are to be revised so that they give more luminous expression to both the nature and the effect of the sacrament."[4]

## Ecclesial Aspects of the Sacrament Rediscovered

As part of this reform, Vatican II also mandated that the faithful be instructed as to the social consequences of sin. Any serious sin is not merely an offense against God, but also has destructive repercussions on the Church and society as a whole. "The role of the Church in penitential practices is not to be passed over, and the people must be exhorted to pray for sinners."[5]

The rites of all the sacraments, including that of Reconciliation, were to be simple, short, and clear, easily understood by the people.[6] To bring about a more active participation of the people in the sacraments and to highlight the connection between the words and rites, there was to be more reading from Holy Scripture.[7] Another important mandate bears quoting:

> It is to be stressed that whenever rites, according to their specific nature, make provision for communal celebration involving the presence and active participation of the faithful, this way of celebrating them is to be preferred, as far as possible, to a celebration that is individual and quasi-private.[8]

This is a mandate to accentuate the base sacrament, the Church, where the people encounter Christ, the primordial Sacrament, whose divinity and humanity through the Incarnation make all other sacramental encounters possible. "Liturgical services are not private functions, but are celebrations of the Church, which is the 'sacrament of unity,' namely, a holy people united and organized under their bishops."[9]

In the Sacrament of Reconciliation, therefore, the penitent is reconciled, through Christ, both to God and to the Church. This is stressed in the *Constitution on the Church (Lumen Gentium):*

> Those who approach the Sacrament of Penance obtain pardon from the mercy of God for offenses committed against him. They are at the same time reconciled with the Church, which they have wounded by their sins, and which by charity, example, and prayer seeks their conversion.[10]

Vatican II issued a call to revise all the sacraments (including that of Reconciliation) in order to accent more this ecclesial dimension, to highlight the importance of hearing the Word of God in Scripture, and to place the emphasis on Jesus as the risen Lord who is encountered in the sacraments. In order to bring out the nature and effects of the individual sacraments more clearly, some freedom was to be allowed for adaptation to various cultures and situations.[11]

## Ordo Penitentiae

The promulgation of the *Rite of Penance* in 1973 was the first great change, both in the theology and in the pastoral administration of Penance since the Council of Trent in the 16th century. This document shows what gigantic steps have been made to carry out the mandates ordered by Vatican II. We can also see its limitations and what elements need further revision for an even greater renewal of this sacrament.

The document is entitled *Ordo Penitentiae.*[12] The word *Penance* has long been used to indicate this sacrament, as in the Councils of Florence (15th century), Trent (16th century) and Vatican II (20th century). At times it is called the Sacrament of Penance and at other times the Sacrament of Reconciliation. Each of the three rites is called individually a *Rite for the Reconciliation* of individual penitents; or of several penitents with individual confession and absolution; and penitents with general confession and absolution. The word *reconciliation* seems to be preferable to *penance* because of its focus on the theme of reconciliation with the Father of mercies through the death and resurrection of his Son by the power of the Holy Spirit through the ministry of the Church.

## New Formulas of Absolution

The acts of the penitent are: contrition, confession, and acts of penance or satisfaction. The most important of these is contrition, heartfelt sorrow and aversion for the sins committed accompanied by the intention of avoiding these sins in the future. Contrition must replace any sense of magic that in earlier times may have been associated with the sacrament because of the emphasis placed on the priest's act of absolution (6). The authenticity of one's inner conversion (*metanoia*) was to be manifested in one's comportment, the modeling of one's whole life on Christ (6a).

The effect of this sacrament is described more as the healing of the roots of sin which lie deeply buried within us, rather than as the juridical absolution of violations of God's commands. Those who by grave sin have broken the communion of love with God are restored to the life they have lost. Frequent and careful celebration of this sacrament can be useful as a remedy for venial sins if there follows a serious striving to perfect the grace of one's Baptism by dying to sin and living a resurrected life in Christ (7b).

The Introduction to the *Ordo Penitentiae* states that the Church exercises the ministry of the Sacrament of Penance through bishops and priests. The document repeats the declarative formula of Trent that the sacrament, by the power of the keys which Christ gave to Peter and handed down through the bishops and priests, is completed by the absolution given by the priest. Yet it also provides for formulas other than the simple form canonized by Trent ("I absolve you from your sins in the name of the Father, and of the Son, and of the Holy Spirit").

The preferred formula of absolution in the three rites is an important improvement over the old one, with deeper roots in Scripture and dogmatic theology. It reads:

> God, the Father of mercies,
> through the death and resurrection of his Son
> has reconciled the world to himself
> and sent the Holy Spirit among us
> for the forgiveness of sins;
> through the ministry of the Church
> may God give you pardon and peace,
> and I absolve you from your sins

in the name of the Father, and of the Son
and of the Holy Spirit.

## Declarative Formula of Absolution

The new prayer of absolution highlights the role of the Trinity to effect reconciliation which is made visible in a ritualized way "through the ministry of the Church." Reconciliation is rightly seen as the gratuitous gift of "the Father of mercies, through the death and resurrection of his Son" and the mediation of the Holy Spirit who was "sent among us for the forgiveness of our sins."

The new rite retains the declarative formula: ". . . and I (the priest) absolve you from your sins." It is unfortunate in my estimation that the framers of this new rite failed to return to the more ancient formula of absolution in which the priest asks, "in the name of the Father, and of the Son, and of the Holy Spirit" that God grant "pardon, peace and absolution" to the penitent. The average penitent, I am afraid, will miss the biblical and theological emphasis on the work of the Trinity as well as the Church's ministry in the process of reconciliation because of the way the new formula of absolution is framed. The members of the committee who worked on the new rite submitted their draft proposal with the bracketed phrase: "[Because of all this], I absolve you. . . ." The absolution of the priest would thus have been connected and subordinated to the true cause of our justification. But unfortunately these words were omitted in the final version.[13]

## Rite I: Reconciliation of Individual Penitents

The Rite of Reconciliation presents three different forms whereby penitents can receive the sacrament. The first rite is not fundamentally different from the rite of private confession canonized in the Council of Trent. However, many secondary elements have been changed to make this traditional form more effective. The Rite consists of eight parts:

1. *Immediate preparation.* Both the priest and the penitent prepare themselves privately. The priest is invited to call upon the Holy Spirit to enlighten him with charity in fulfilling his role. The penitent is encouraged to spend some time in examining his or her life in light of the example and commands of Christ in the Gospel. In intimate, personal prayer, he or she begs God to forgive any sins committed and to heal the roots of those sins.

2. *Reception of the penitent.* The priest is encouraged to greet the penitent with warmth and friendliness. To facilitate this, there has been introduced in most Roman Catholic parishes the "Reconciliation Room." The penitent has a choice to remain in hidden anonymity behind a screen, or can choose to meet the confessor face to face.

3. *Reading of the Word of God.* This element was mandated in Vatican II's *Constitution on the Sacred Liturgy.*[14] But it can be made optional, especially if there is a long line of penitents seeking reconciliation. The value of meditating on God's Word is to open one's heart to a deeper experience of his love and mercy.

4. *Confession of sins.* The value of a personal confession of sins is to bring to the light of God's love and mercy what has been hidden in the darkness of one's heart and life. It is essential to the valid reception of the sacrament to be specific in the cases of grave sins. Hence one should confess all sins with the number of times they were committed, and with any details necessary for the priest to be able to offer the proper advice as to how to avoid them in the future and grow in the likeness of the risen Christ. Those who choose individual confession out of devotion should look at trends, elements, and roots that can be exposed and guarded against, for the sake of greater

81

growth in holiness of life. In such a context, the priest can be of great assistance by offering spiritual direction and encouragement.

5. *The imposition and acceptance of a penance.* The priest then imposes a penance. Prayers are frequently assigned, but more and more often the penance has to do with repairing the damage caused by the sins committed by performing contrary acts: doing a specific good deed for someone who may have injured you, for example. The penance should be accepted in a spirit of good will and performed with the attitude that it will contribute to one's overall growth in love.

6. *Prayer of the penitent.* Most Catholics have memorized an act of contrition which expresses their sorrow for having offended the goodness of God in the past and includes an expression of their firm determination to avoid sin in the future. Suggested additional forms of prayers of sorrow are found in #85-92 of the document. Spontaneous prayers of repentance are encouraged.

7. *Absolution.* The new formula of absolution is recited by the priest. It shows the connection between the reconciliation of the sinner and the initiative of God who, through the death and resurrection of his Son and the sending of the Holy Spirit, has made such reconciliation possible through the ministry of the Church. The priest says the words of absolution "in persona Christi," that is to say, the priest forgives the penitent's sins, not personally, but in the place of Christ, with the authority to do so given him by the Church.

8. *Proclamation of praise and dismissal of the penitent.* Both priest and penitent give thanks and praise to God for his boundless mercy in granting pardon and peace to the penitent in the sacrament. The penitent is encouraged to continue living according to the Gospel precepts of love for God and neighbor.

## Rite II: Reconciliation of Several Penitents with Individual Confession and Absolution

This is a rite which stands mid-way between individual confession and private absolution (Rite I) and general absolution of several penitents with no specific confession of sins (Rite III). It adds to the First Rite a sense of the very real relationship which exists between the repentant sinner and the ecclesial community. There is a social aspect to sin. Sinners affect the Church and the world.[15] This rite came into being in answer to the mandate of Vatican II to provide for the presence and active participation of the faithful in the sacraments, since a communal celebration "is to be preferred, as far as possible, to a celebration that is individual and quasi-private."[16]

There are six main parts of Rite II:[17]

1. The communal service begins with *a gathering song* to foster a sense of unity in heart and mind among the participants (#23). The words of the song are to prepare the members of the community to assimilate the Word of God and receive his forgiving mercy.

2. *Greeting of the priest* (#49; 94-96). A brief explanation of the importance and purpose of the gathering is given to remove any fear or anxiety and to explain the clear and simple elements that make up the service. The priest prays for repentance on behalf of the community (#15, 50, 97-100).

3. *Celebration of the Word of God* (#24). One or more readings from Sacred Scripture are chosen. These express in concrete ways how God is always ready to forgive when sinners turn to him with humble and contrite hearts.

4. After the *examination of conscience*, all participants recite a prayer which acknowledges their sinfulness (#27). They then join in a litany or fitting song to express their heartfelt contrition and trust in God's mercy. This part ends with the *recitation of the Lord's Prayer*, which is never omitted.

5. *Confession.* Penitents who want to confess their sins go to the priest of their choice and do so. They accept the penance given by the priest and receive his absolution. It is evident from the length of the service plus the number of penitents wishing to confess privately that such confessions must be made as briefly as possible. This seems to have been behind the intention expressed in #55: "Everything else which is customary in individual confession is omitted."

6. *Proclamation of praise* (#29) *and dismissal* (#30). When all confessions have been heard, the priests return to the sanctuary. The presiding priest invites all to give thanks in prayer to God and to praise him for his mercy manifested in the rite of Reconciliation. This is usually done through the recitation of a psalm or the singing of a hymn. The priest then concludes with a prayer thanking God for his infinite love and mercy.

### Difficulties Created by Rite II

Several difficulties present themselves in this rite. One concerns the feasibility of bringing together several confessors for the service. There would be a "rushed" feeling among priests to dispense absolution without giving much counsel or encouragement, even if these were sorely needed by the penitent. Penitents who had been away from this sacrament for a long time would need help to examine their conscience and little time is available. They would also require special assistance and encouragement to make a firm proposal to amend their life in the future.

Penitents not in serious sin would tend to reduce their confession to generalities instead of dealing with the root causes of their failings. They would probably receive little if any spiritual direction to suit their particular needs.

Then there is the problem of the obligatory nature of receiving absolution from a priest in Rite II, whether or not one has sinned grievously. Would there be scandal if one did not (or did) approach a priest for absolution?

## *Rite III: Reconciliation of Penitents with General Absolution*

Rite III is to be used only in cases of emergency (possible imminent death, for example) or in other pastoral situations determined by the local bishop in keeping with the policies set by the national or regional conferences of bishops. It is to be used only in rare and predetermined exceptional cases.

It should be pointed out that there were some persons on the two committees that framed this rite who wanted to restrict the use of general absolution to "last resort" situations, while others sought to extend its use to apply especially to the faithful not habitually committing serious sins. The Sacrament of Reconciliation would thus become available on a regular basis to the majority of the faithful while the use of individual private confession and absolution (Rite I) would be frequented principally by those who were in serious sin or wanted to avail themselves of the exceptional grace-filled opportunity for personal spiritual direction which this form provides.

### *Celebration of Rite III*

The celebration of this rite follows the same form given in Rite II. However, after the homily the priest explains the dispositions necessary to receive this sacrament properly. Then some sort of general penance is imposed on all. The penitents are encouraged to add to the general penance a penance of their own choosing, according to their circumstances and the movement of grace.

The priest then extends his hands over the penitents and recites the prayer(s) of absolution found in #62. In the suggested Prayers for General Absolution, we see a return to the *imperative* formula of the early Church in which the Father, Son and Spirit are implored to grant mercy and reconciliation to the penitents. These prayers, however, conclude with the *declarative* formula of Trent: "And I absolve you from your sins in the name of the Father and of the Son and of the Holy Spirit." The other new formula of absolution found in Rites I and II is also suggested as an option, again with the declarative formula as its conclusion.

The rite ends with a proclamation of praise and the priest's blessing followed by the dismissal of the people (#35d).


## Summary and Conclusions

Great positive steps have been made in the three new rites of the *Ordo Penitentiae*. The Holy Spirit is obviously working to renew the sacrament through these three rites. Hence their promulgation should be considered a special grace reserved for our own day and age. At the same time, we must continue to be open to the possibility, indeed to the hope, that in the future even richer rites will be promulgated.

All three rites reconcile penitents, but use two different forms, namely through private auricular confession, and through the communal penitential service. In both forms, priestly absolution is given — either to an individual or to a group. The *Ordo Penitentiae* shows that all three rites are lawful ways of receiving the Sacrament of Reconciliation.

Rite I is intended both for the reconciliation of grievous sinners and for those persons who do not need absolution of serious sins, but find in private, auricular confession the "locus" of a deeper, more personal encounter with their merciful and forgiving Savior.

Rite II stresses the social aspects of sin and brings individual penitents into the healing and reconciling atmosphere of a loving community as the base sacrament which "incarnates" Christ in our day and age as God's reconciling love for us.

Rite III of all the rites has caused the greatest confusion since it is concerned with general absolution of all sins, mortal and venial, with no immediate private confession to a priest. There is an unspoken but underlying fear that general absolution might eliminate or lessen the demand for private confession and individual absolution. This is surely at the basis of so many restrictions placed on this rite. For that reason the explanation of this rite begins with the Tridentine teaching that "individual, integral confession and absolution remain the only ordinary way for the faithful to reconcile themselves with God and the Church, unless physical or moral impossibility excuses from this kind of confession" (#31). This statement assumes that *the ordinary model* of Reconciliation is that of absolution from *serious* sins. But pastorally, we know that this is not true. Most of the faithful do not live in mortal sin and ordinarily approach the sacrament for the grace and peace which it provides. If that is the case, and I sincerely believe it is, then the *ordinary rite of Reconciliation* would take care of the needs of those with *venial* sins on their souls. Would not Rites I and II, in this scenario, then, be considered extraordinary and Rite III the usual way for the faithful to receive the Sacrament of Reconciliation? To limit Rite III to exceptional cases (cf. #31-32) seems to me to be pastorally, if not theologically, flawed.

With these thoughts in mind, let us turn next to the important matter of general absolution in the context of Rite III, to see whether it may in the future be legitimately considered as an *ordinary* way to validly receive the Sacrament of Reconciliation.

Chapter Seven

# COMMUNAL SERVICE OF RECONCILIATION

*A State of General Confusion*

For thirty years I have been constantly engaged in preaching retreats and missions in parishes, convents, monasteries and retreat houses. This has brought me into vital contact with both clergy and laity in regard to the new rites of Reconciliation promulgated in 1973 (in the United States in 1975). Generally, both the clergy and their parishioners seem to be confused about the new rites. In 1983, the National Conference of Catholic Bishops gave the following assessment of their acceptance:

> Although intensive study and discussion preceded formulation of the revised Rite of Penance, pastoral problems continue to surround the sacrament. The new rites of Reconciliation emphasize the reality of both personal and social sin in the Christian community and affirm that Christians are reconciled with God through the ministry of the Church. The fact is, however, that the importance of this sacrament has declined in the lives of many Christians, who are not likely to recover appreciation for it unless they are once again convinced of its role in their lives.[1]

## Lack of Implementation

In speaking to parishioners around the country, I have been amazed at how few even know about the three new rites. The average parishioner knows only that there is now a choice to confess one's sins face to face rather than behind the veiled grate of the confessional, and that the confessor now uses a new formula for absolution.

Initially there was a genuine if not whole-hearted effort on the part of most pastors to provide a catechesis for their parishioners when the rites were first approved. They were often assisted in this by the printed material which the liturgical commissions of the various dioceses made available. But little enthusiasm was generated for the new changes, possibly because the Sacrament of Reconciliation was the last rite to be renewed and many priests and lay people in the parishes were exhausted from the introduction of so many innovations in the way they celebrated the sacraments. Another more serious reason might be that the new forms place greater demands on both confessor and penitent, requiring greater interiority, prayer in one another's presence, an attempt to get at the hidden areas of one's life which might be at the root of one's brokenness and sin, and a genuine resolve to amend one's conduct.

## Norms Issued by the Vatican

Since 1973, the Vatican has issued a number of restrictions in the uses of Forms II and III. Bishops the world over, even before the rites were promulgated, had asked the Holy See for clarifications, especially concerning Form III: communal liturgical celebration of the sacrament with general absolution.

According to the Norms issued in 1972 (*Sacramentum paenitentiae*), Form III with general absolution was to be used only in exceptional circumstances, to be determined by the National or Regional Conferences of Bishops and not by individual pastors.[2]

Throughout these Norms, Rites II and III are spoken of as

extraordinary forms to be used "in grave necessity," while Rite I was to be considered the "ordinary" form, based on the Tridentine decrees concerning integral confession.[3]

Pope Paul VI in an allocution to some American bishops in 1978 gave the current thinking of the Vatican on the use of general absolution: "It is permitted only for the *extraordinary* situations of *grave necessity* as indicated in Norm III. Just last year we drew attention publicly to the altogether exceptional character of general absolution . . . We ask for a faithful observance of these norms."[4]

The Synod of Bishops, called for by Pope John Paul II in 1983, a decade after the promulgation of the new Rite, discussed ways of bringing the faithful back to more frequent reception of the sacrament. John Paul II, at the end of the Synod in his apostolic exhortation of December 2, 1984, again categorically affirmed that for a Christian the Sacrament of Penance is "the ordinary way of obtaining forgiveness and the remission of serious sins committed after Baptism."[5] He then went on to add:

> The first form — reconciliation of individual penitents — is the *only normal* and *ordinary* way of celebrating the Sacrament, and it cannot and must not be allowed to fall into disuse or to be neglected.[6]

*Present State of the Sacrament*

The official, "ordinary" form of confession preferred and encouraged by the Holy See is the private auricular confession of sins as found in Form I. This is geared to absolve grievous sinners from mortal sins by the power given to the confessor. Some pastoral problems arise when it is applied to those who wish to frequent this sacrament and yet have not committed serious sins. All of the papal documents from Trent to the present day encourage the pious laity to frequent the Sacrament of Reconciliation or Penance. But we must ask ourselves, "Why do so many ordinary penitents no longer frequent this form?" Most confessors will readily admit that many penitents have little or no experience of true reconciliation in private confession.

If the "ordinary" form of confession is not ordinarily being used by Roman Catholics in any significant number, what can we say about the "extraordinary" Forms, II and III? Form II is an uncomfortable compromise between private confession and a communal penance service because in this rite, there is little or no time in the period set aside for private confession for the penitent to deal in any depth with his or her sins and the general state of their spiritual health. The shortage of priests also tends to rule out wide-spread use of this Second Form in most parishes. The length of the service where there is a large number of penitents waiting to go to confession has also been a deterrent. And we have already pointed out that Form III has been reduced by the Holy See to use only in case of grave necessity and as a last resort.

## Different Needs Demand Different Rituals

Communal celebrations meet needs different from those met by private individual confession. There is no question of opposing one form to the other. Both forms are needed.[7] Communal penance services enable us, in the community of caring fellow Christians, to move from the *heteronomous* level (where we relate to God as law-giver and punisher) and from the *autonomous* level (where *we* determine our relationship with God and what constitutes sin for *us)* to the *theonomous* level (where God is the complete Center and Ground of our being).

Such services can lead us into an honest realization of our own individual as well as social brokenness and sin. Reconciliation is experienced as a process of ongoing conversion within a community, for only in community where we are supported by the love of others can we find the strength to dare to undertake the deeper levels of conversion to which God may be calling us, a conversion which may require a complete change of lifestyle.

In communal penance services we come to a greater appreciation of the evil of sin and its deleterious effects on our relationship
with God and neighbor. We recognize it for the obstacle it is to God's
being more fully active in our life.

## Non-Sacramental Means of Reconciliation

There are a number of human situations in which people receive the
grace of repentance, forgiveness and reconciliation outside the
seven sacraments. When the Council of Trent in the 16th century
defined and named the seven sacraments, it did not intend to imply
that they are the only means by which God's grace comes to us.
Many non-sacramental acts and rituals extend the effects of the
sacraments to us. A wife patiently taking care of her husband
afflicted with Alzheimer's disease is living out the sacrament they
originally celebrated on their wedding day. We can easily apply this
to the Sacrament of Reconciliation. Today all of us see that reconciliation is taking place under the power of the Holy Spirit in many so-
called ordinary situations: in the work-place, at home, at school,
between husband and wife, parents and children, friend and neighbor, and so forth. Under the inspiration of the Holy Spirit, "nations
even seek the way of peace together" (*Eucharistic Prayer for Masses
of Reconciliation II*).

Communal penitential celebrations, which the Norms of 1972
describe as non-sacramental, can be helpful to foster the spirit of
penance within the Christian community. "Penitential celebrations,
moreover, are very useful in places where no priest is available to
give sacramental absolution. They often help in reaching that
perfect contrition which comes from charity and enables the faithful
to attain to God's grace through a desire for the Sacrament of
Penance."[8]

Such services can also be offered occasionally as a form of
inculcating both a new sense of responsibility for our life in the
present as well as greater sorrow for past failures. This could be

done simply to make parishioners aware of their individual and communal solidarity as well as of their mutual "sinfulness." These non-sacramental penitential services must always be measured by how much they help parishioners to be more open to the graces of the Sacrament of Reconciliation itself.

## Healing of Memories

Another non-sacramental form of reconciliation with God and neighbor is the healing of memories which often takes place in charismatic prayer services. Again, its great value is the gathering together in love of a group of caring persons to praise God in Jesus through the Holy Spirit in an atmosphere of prayer. In such a setting, people can enter into areas of past hurts, bring them to the light and healing touch of Jesus in prayer, and be comforted by the loving support and prayers of their brothers and sisters in the community. Often such a service becomes a stimulus for an individual to seek out sacramental Reconciliation.

## Examination of Conscience

One manner of developing a deeper awareness of sin and our need for God's grace is the daily discipline of the examination of conscience. This exercise is vital for those truly serious in growing in greater agapic love for God and neighbor.[9]

Both in receiving the Sacrament of Reconciliation and in the daily performance of this exercise, we are led to greater self-knowledge and are moved to be more honest and humble as we call on God's continued mercy.

The five steps in such a service of accountability before the Trinity that St. Ignatius of Loyola offers in his *Spiritual Exercises* are most applicable and profitable to us today. These steps serve as a mini-judgment, made by ourselves, on who we are by examining the quality of our thoughts, words and deeds of a given day.

94

*Step One*:  We give praise and thanksgiving to God for all his many gifts bestowed upon each of us from the beginning of time to today.

*Step Two*:  We pray to the Father and the Son that in the love and wisdom of the Spirit we may honestly see our sins and omissions in thought, word and deed.

*Step Three*:  In union with the Trinity we see ourselves as God sees us, with humility and honesty and a total desire to make God the sole Center of our life. We review our waking moments, activities, and relationships with others in all we did that day. We see the goodness of God and our responses to his infinite love and mercy.

*Step Four*:  We cry out before the majesty of God for the healing power of the risen Lord Jesus to come into the broken relationships of that day. We beg that his transforming light and love might dispel the darkness of our self-centeredness. We long that he lay his healing hands upon our blindness in failing to have been more aware of his presence in all moments of the day. May he again say *"Ephphatha!"* and open our ears to his strengthening and encouraging Word.

*Step Five*:  We offer to the loving Trinity the gift of tomorrow to be lived in greater intimacy and self-surrendering love to their immanent presence in us and around us that we might live as faithful, worshipful children of so loving a God.


*Communal Penance Services for Children*

When St. Pope Pius X lowered the age for children to receive the Eucharist in his decree, *Quam singulari*,[10] the common practice followed that children had first to receive the Sacrament of Penance. This, of course, has been administered in the usual rite of private confession.

This practice has been challenged in our day by developments in child psychology, and in sacramental and pastoral theology.[11] The argument generally set forward is that neither children nor adults are obliged to confess venial sins in order to receive the Eucharist. Nonetheless, children at the early age of six and seven are prepared for a rite designed for the absolution of mortal sins. This can tend to create a sense of guilt disproportionate to the faults committed which can plague an individual throughout his or her life. It can also reinforce the idea that sins are external violations of laws and rules rather than the betrayal of a personal relationship with God and neighbor. Such an approach would be superficial in that it ignores the deeper underlying reasons behind any evil doing.

Having said all this, let us also concede the considerable wisdom on the part of the Church in insisting that children be prepared to receive the Sacrament of Reconciliation before their First Communion (Canon 777, #2). Children know when they have done wrong and offended God, their parents, their teachers, their brothers and sisters, their classmates. They feel guilty and want to feel good about themselves again. They want to have their hurt relationships healed. As I mentioned at the beginning of this book, I look back fondly on those days of my youth when confession was a regular part of my life. No child should be denied, nor should they lightly pass up, the experience of lightness, warmth and peace which washes over you when you hear Jesus, in the person of the priest, say to you that your sins have been forgiven you. The world seems brighter and you are filled with joy when you are reconciled to the Father through the Spirit in the gentle love of the merciful Lord.

All Catholics — including children — should know how to approach the Sacrament of Reconciliation, in all of its three forms, and what to expect when doing so. Children, therefore, *should* be taught how to confess their sins to a priest, though they should probably not be obliged to do so until they feel ready, since the law itself does not require it. There are other equally valid ways to receive the Sacrament of Reconciliation. For most young children, a communal penance service modeled on Form III might be a pastorally and psychologically better way to introduce them to the sacrament.

## Two Forms of Reconciliation

Form II of the new Rite of Reconciliation (communal penance service combined with private confession), as we have said, is a compromise between Form I (private confession with individual absolution) and Form III (communal penance service with general absolution). Thus we can see that there now exist in the Catholic Church two forms of liturgical, sacramental forgiveness of sins: private and communal.

I believe that Christians will eventually recognize both of these forms as "ordinary" and equally accepted ways of receiving the Sacrament of Reconciliation. Each rite offers particular advantages which meet the different needs of a variety of penitents.

There are times when penitents feel the need for privacy, especially to claim one's personal sins and sinfulness before a priest who can incarnate a deeply personal encounter with Jesus Christ as compassionate healer and guide. Other penitents may feel that they derive sufficient benefit from receiving the Sacrament of Reconciliation in a communal service that makes them vitally aware of their guilt before God and their brothers and sisters in community. Such an encounter may lead them from the communal, social setting to desire an even more personal encounter with the Lord in private confession.

These two forms should never be seen as competing with one another but rather as richly complementary to one another.

## Problems Associated with Both Forms

We must acknowledge that in both rites penitents can drift into a mentality of magical expectancy that a true reconciliation with God can be accomplished without hard work, repentance, and a real conversion of life. Confessors frequently lament the few penitents who use Form I compared with the relatively large numbers of parishioners who attend general, communal penance services, especially during Lent and Advent. We need to remember that the communal service is not superior because it is more popular. Some may seek general absolution simply because it is easier. They do not have to manifest their consciences or even delve very deeply into the roots of their own sinfulness. Such people reason that general absolution will accomplish a reconciliation with God with the least amount of personal discomfort. But there are others who find in a communal penance service a powerful encounter with the Lord that fosters a true change of heart and an ongoing reform of their daily life.

The main disadvantage facing those who prefer Form I, private confession, is that they may expect some kind of magical increase of grace just because they rotely confess their usual list of venial sins and are present as the priest absolves them.

Let us now turn to some examples of communal penance services in order to show some of the richness available in this reconciling sacrament of God's mercy.

Chapter Eight

# THE CELEBRATION OF
# COMMUNAL PENANCE SERVICES

*True Repentance and the Holy Spirit*

Repentance, as Jesus announced in the "good news" of the Gospel, is the transformation of sinful individual existence into the Kingdom of God where we participate in the very life of God himself (2 P 1:4). It is the work of the Church to preach repentance. In Greek, repentance is *metanoia*, which refers to a conversion or upheaval of our habitual ways of thinking and doing, and implies a "change of heart and mind," the putting on of new attitudes and values which transform the old into a "new creation in Christ" (2 Cor 5:17).

Baptized into the Trinitarian community of God through the grace of the living, risen Christ, our Head, we Christians are still caught between two forces: the power of evil and the Spirit of Christ, the unspiritual in us and the spiritual. The Spirit has created this new life within us, fosters it, stimulates its growth, purifies us from any obstacle to its maturity and brings this life to its fullness in the proportion that we allow him to be the normative influence in our lives, guiding us in all those moral choices which impact on our true growth in Christ.

The Spirit frees us from fear and anxiety, and helps us to overcome that aggressiveness which causes us to try to control and possess others as "things." He teaches us to love with a love that is more divine than human. That which was impossible to us humanly becomes possible through the Spirit who fashions us into a unique image of Jesus Christ, who is himself the Image of the Father.

The Spirit is the creative, transforming power of God that is always uniting what is divided. Where more profoundly can this transformation take place than in a community of penitents humbly crying out for communal and individual forgiveness? The freedom which the Spirit gives is never the license to do whatever we please, but rather consists in the total submission of our entire being to the authority of God: "In Christ you who heard the word of truth — the good news of your salvation — and believed it were sealed by the promised Holy Spirit, which is the pledge that we shall gain our inheritance when God redeems what he has acquired, to the praise of his glory" (Ep 1:13-14).

## History of Communal Penance Services

Many French Catholic priests in the 1950's felt dissatisfied with the lack of preparation for the reception of the Sacrament of Reconciliation and came up with the idea of using communal liturgies as a means to remedy this situation while at the same time providing instruction in moral formation for their parishioners. Such services were designed to create a more authentic sense of sin and to lead the participants to a more profound desire to do penance and reform their lives. Vatican II encouraged the development of such services.[1]

For good Christians, serious about living dynamic lives of prayer, asceticism, and good works, a communal penance service was an ideal complement to private confession. In these services greater emphasis was placed on the unique, human potential of each penitent in his or her vital relationship with God and other human beings in the context of the ecclesial experience of being one with other members of the Body of Christ.

At the same time, these communal services offered the opportunity, to those whose hearts had been set aflame by the fire of divine love, to receive the Sacrament of Reconciliation.

## The Church's Role in Reconciliation

Without an inner, personal relationship between the penitent and God in his Church, the Body of Christ, there can be no authentic *sacramental* encounter with Christ, who is the primordial Reconciler of sinners to the Father through the Holy Spirit. The Church's role in the Sacrament of Reconciliation is to foster in the hearts of penitents this more personal relationship with the Lord by helping the penitent to develop a conscience informed by God's revelation in Scripture and in the teachings of the Church.[2]

The new rite emphasizes the centrality of the paschal mystery of Christ and the importance of the action of the Holy Spirit.[3] This is in keeping with the Church's constant endeavor to bring the Holy Spirit into the center of Christian life, especially in the celebration of the sacraments. Godfrey Dieckmann, O.S.B., has written: "The post-conciliar liturgical reform will help us rediscover the Holy Spirit."[4]

Another key point stressed by the Church in the new rite is the role of the confessor as a healing physician, and not principally as a judge. In the text of the new rite, in fact, the Sacrament of Penance is referred to more than twenty times as a healing ministry mediated by a confessor, the image of judge being found only twice.

The term "Reconciliation" expresses more accurately than the term "Penance" the idea of the sinner's being reconnected to God and to the Church through this sacrament. This communal aspect of the sacrament was largely lost when the Celtic form of private confession was universally accepted as the only rite for Roman Catholics. In the new rite, this aspect has been restored in such prayers as this which the individual penitent is invited to recite: "Forgive my sins, renew your love in my heart; help me to live in perfect unity with my fellow Christians that I may proclaim your saving power to the world."[5]

The new rite also specifies that "communal celebration shows more fully the ecclesial nature of penance."[6] It is in large part for this reason that the celebration of the Sacrament of Reconciliation in the presence of the community is almost universally the norm in the Eastern Rite Christian Churches. Moreover, all three forms — private confession (I), communal celebration with individual confession and absolution (II), and communal celebration with general absolution (III) — are also practiced in the various Eastern Churches.

## A Suggested Form of Communal Reconciliation

Having been ordained in the Russian Byzantine Rite as a Catholic priest and having for thirty years preached retreats and missions around the country, I have always felt comfortable with the three forms of the new rite since they have all been available in most of the Eastern Christian Churches, both Catholic and Orthodox, over the years. I myself have evolved a communal penance and healing service for both Roman and Byzantine Catholic congregations. In the context of the Liturgy of St. John Chrysostom, the Sacrament of Reconciliation is celebrated with general absolution. I present this as a true sacrament for those not living in serious sins, while those in grievous sin are encouraged to build upon this service as a preparation for private confession and individual absolution with a confessor.

The locus of Reconciliation from earliest times has always been within the Church-community, climaxed in the Eucharist, the ritualized peak of God's forgiving and healing love through the Holy Spirit in Jesus Christ as the Bread of Life.

## Format of the Celebration

This liturgical celebration takes about two hours since, for a meaningful and fruitful celebration of deep repentance and conversion before God's infinite triune forgiveness and healing love, more than the basic minimum is required. Examination of one's sinfulness and

102

the celebration of our healing from sin, both communal and individual, is a process that takes place through the use of archetypal symbols, incense, meditative readings, reflections on the Beatitudes, a homily and exhortative prayers, the laying on of hands, and an anointing by the priest accompanied by the impetrative prayer that Jesus bring his healing and absolving power to each penitent in God's community of love.

Meaningful liturgy cannot be rushed. Human nature does not make an abrupt transition into the living presence of the invisible Trinity. Such a celebration should be considered a seasonal ritual, administered during Lent, Advent, and other liturgically significant times of the year according to the discretion of the pastor and the needs of the community. Reconciliation is a celebration that demands preparation and time on the part of the celebrant as well as the penitents. When such a celebration is carefully planned and prepared by both the confessors and the penitents, all will experience a ritual that is prayerful, moving, edifying and effective. And it will proceed smoothly and expeditiously.

## Explanation

This event should normally take place in the evening in order to take maximum advantage of the symbols of darkness and light. It is divided into three distinct parts, one flowing into the other, with the climax of healing and reconciliation being reached in the Eucharist:

1. The Penance and Healing Service
2. Liturgy of the Word
3. The Eucharistic Canon

The priest begins by greeting the faithful who have gathered to seek both communal and individual reconciliation with God and with one another. He outlines the flow of the service, so that without too much shuffling of papers and use of books the entire congregation can participate in the service in a spirit of oneness with the celebrant and the other penitents.

The priest will seek to instruct the faithful in the aim of the service and lead them to a deeper, more scriptural sense of sin. For those not living in grievous sin, the emphasis will be on the need for healing and reconciliation rather than on disclosing every last venial fault. The priest will seek to lead those bound by serious sin to true sorrow for their willful alienation from a loving heavenly Father, that they might be open to extend this service in the form of private confession. At that point, they may privately and integrally confess all serious sins against God and neighbor, and arrive at a more perfect sorrow and firm amendment through individual absolution by a priest.

A suggested penance service is outlined as follows.

A COMMUNAL HEALING AND PENANCE SERVICE

1. With the lights on, the community sings a hymn that will set the tone for hearing God's call to his chosen people to come back to him with all their hearts. All the main lights are then turned off, with essentially only seven candles in a candelabra on the main altar glowing in the dark.
2. The priest prays and invites all to repentance.
3. This is followed by a reading from Isaiah 1:2-10, 18-20. The first reader uses the light of a flashlight or small lamp at the pulpit.
4. Next the priest leads the people through a reflective examination of conscience, along the lines of the eight Beatitudes followed by a penitential litany drawn from Gospel stories and values.

*A. Examen According to the Eight Beatitudes*

Celebrant:   May you be blessed, O Lord, for having promised the Kingdom of Heaven to those who have the spirit of poverty. Pardon us for our excessive attachment to money, to comforts, and to creatures at the cost of our attachment to you, and for failing to share as stewards your gifts to us with the needy whom we have met or learned about.

[Pause: Let each reflect on how he or she may have failed to live this Beatitude.]

Celebrant and penitents all together respond: "As we forgive one another, forgive us, O Lord."

Celebrant:     May you be blessed, O Lord, for having promised your inheritance to those who are kind and gentle. Pardon us for being impatient with others, especially in our families, in our parish, and at our work. Pardon our hostility toward those who disagree with us, who are not of our kind.

[Pause]

All:              As we forgive one another, forgive us, O Lord.

Celebrant:     May you be blessed, O Lord, for having offered your divine consolation to those who are afflicted. Pardon us for seeking consolation in anything but you, and for neglecting to comfort others when we saw their needs, especially the homeless, the hungry, the depressed and dejected.

[Pause]

All:              As we forgive one another, forgive us, O Lord.

Celebrant:     May you be blessed, O Lord, for you satisfy those who hunger and thirst for justice. Pardon us for considering ourselves better than others, and for not having the courage to take an unpopular stand when justice seemed to require it, and pardon us for our convenient disregard for the truth.

[Pause]

All:          As we forgive one another, forgive us, O Lord.

Celebrant:   Blessed are you, O Lord, for you show mercy to the merciful. Pardon us for not forgiving others as true Christians must —at home, in our parish, at work, at recreation, in our community. For our lack of compassion toward the broken ones of this world.

[Pause]

All:          As we forgive one another, forgive us, O Lord.

Celebrant:   Blessed are you, O Lord, because you show yourself to the pure of heart. Pardon us for our lack of sincerity with you and with our neighbor . . . and for the misuse of all the good and holy things you have given us, especially in the misuse of our time and our talents.

[Pause]

All:          As we forgive one another, forgive us, O Lord.

Celebrant:   May you be blessed, O Lord, for promising peace to women and men of good will. Pardon us, O Lord, for our divisiveness and our lack of understanding which has caused the destruction of peace both in our personal, daily lives and in our community.

[Pause]

All:          As we forgive one another, forgive us, O Lord.

Celebrant:   May you be blessed, O Lord, for promising the Kingdom of Heaven to those who suffer for the cause of right. Pardon us for complaining . . . for not seeing your holy presence in our personal troubles . . . for not proclaiming our belief in your goodness through every trial we experience.

## B. Penitential Litany

Celebrant: With the publican of the Gospel, let us say . . .

All: O God, be merciful to me, a sinner!

Celebrant: You go to meet the prodigal son; you clasp him in your arms and kiss him . . .

All: O God, be merciful to me, a sinner!

Celebrant: You accept the ointment of the sinful woman; because of her tears you pardon her . . .

All: O God, be merciful to me, a sinner!

Celebrant: You choose as your apostle, the tax collector Matthew; you have not come to call the righteous but sinners . . .

All: O God, be merciful to me, a sinner!

Celebrant: To the good thief who implores you, you open the gate of paradise . . .

All: O God, be merciful to me, a sinner!

Celebrant: For the many expressions of luxury which we invite into our lives, thereby distracting us from you, the true Center of our life, we beg you . . .

All: O God, be merciful to me, a sinner!

Celebrant: For the times we have chosen the ways of the world over your ways, O Lord, we beg you . . .

All: O God, be merciful to me, a sinner!

Celebrant: For the sinful use of our tongue, we beg you . . .

All: O God, be merciful to me, a sinner!

Celebrant: For the times we have purposely escaped mentally from being fully and consciously present and participating in the Eucharist, we beg you . . .

All: O God, be merciful to me, a sinner!

Celebrant: For avoiding responsibility and our fair share of work in our family, parish, at work, in our community, we beg you . . .

All: O God, be merciful to me, a sinner!

Celebrant: For showing others, especially the young, the image of a bored and apathetic Christian, we beg you . . .

All: O God, be merciful to me, a sinner!

Celebrant: For our many sins against charity, especially in not concerning ourselves with the plight of the poor and unfortunate ones around us, we beg you . . .

All: O God, be merciful to me, a sinner!

Celebrant: For the times we have failed to pray and be present to you, we beg you . . .

All: O God, be merciful to me, a sinner!

Celebrant: For our failure to curb habitual sins, we beg you . . .

All: O God, be merciful to me, a sinner!

Celebrant: For our excessive love of self, we beg you . . .

All: O God, be merciful to me, a sinner!

Celebrant: Let us pray. Almighty and merciful God, how wonderfully you created man and woman, and still more wonderfully remake them. You do not abandon the sinner but seek him out with a father's love. You sent your Son into this world to destroy sin and death by his passion and to restore life and joy by his resurrection. You constantly renew our spirit in the sacraments of your redeeming love, freeing us from slavery to sin and transforming us ever more closely into the likeness of your beloved Son, who lives and reigns with you in the unity of the Holy Spirit, one God, forever and ever. Amen.

5. The celebrant then puts incense upon lighted coals in a brazier or bowl, holds it up as he stands before the altar

facing the people, and chants aloud the first words of Psalm 141: "Let my prayer rise like incense; the lifting up of my hands like an evening sacrifice." He then announces the second reader who meditatively reads the penitential Psalm 51 of King David.

During this reading the priest goes down among the faithful and holds out the incense bowl. The faithful hold their hands reverently over the bowl and raise them upward in a symbol of purification from sin and total surrender to God as a gift of self.

6. The celebrant prayerfully begins the healing of memories by leading the participants through their life, beginning with the very first moment of conception. Such healing of memories should be done peacefully and with confidence that Jesus can heal all broken relationships of the past and present. The celebrant proposes areas of brokenness, dysfunctionalism, anything that may constitute an obstacle preventing a penitent from being free to live a loving Christian life. He will have to suggest elements in the lives of penitents who may represent married, single, or celibate persons (celibate in the sense of an ordained priest or member of a religious congregation observing the evangelical counsels of poverty, chastity and obedience). He will seek to touch on the relationships of early childhood, even from the womb, brought about by one's genetic pre-programming or relationships in the formative years, in adolescence, in the decade of one's twenties, thirties, forties, fifties, and old age, down to the present moment.

The priest, humbly but with confidence, calls upon Jesus the Lord to come as Divine Healer and Reconciler to heal and make whole the penitents who now call upon his name and desire to enter into an intimate encounter with him as Lord and Savior. The celebrant then, with blessed oil (but not that used for the Anointing of the Sick), anoints the penitents as they approach him or other assisting priests in line. As he anoints the forehead of each individual, the priest prays the impetrative prayer of healing and absolution: "May our Lord Jesus Christ heal you of all your infirmities of body, soul, and spirit, and absolve you of all your sins, in the name of the Father and of the Son and of the Holy Spirit."

During the anointing there should be special music to inspire a deeper spirit of confidence in God's infinite mercy and forgiveness, that the healing power of Jesus will bring about a new and ongoing conversion in the heart of the individual penitent and within the community at large.

When all have been anointed, the celebrant prays over the entire congregation that there be reconciliation in that community as well as other communities important to each individual such as immediate family, relatives, ancestors, even the city, state, country, and earth that we all share.

The congregation sings: "Lord, have mercy; Christ, have mercy; Lord, have mercy." The priest then concludes this part of the Penance Service with the words: "Go in peace. Jesus Christ has set you free!"

THE LITURGY OF THE WORD

1. The third reader reads the very dramatic *Reverse Creation* (below). We have just surrendered our sinfulness to God and, as we prepare to hear with joy of the cosmic redemption of Christ in the next reading, we must here recall the cosmic brokenness around us:

*Reverse Creation*

In the end, we destroyed the heaven that was called Earth. The Earth had been beautiful until our spirit moved over it and destroyed all things.

And we said . . .

Let there be darkness . . . and there was darkness. And we liked the darkness; so we called the darkness, Security. And we divided ourselves into races and religions and classes of society. And there was no morning and no evening on the seventh day before the end.

And we said . . .

Let there be a strong government to control us in our darkness. Let there be armies to control our bodies so that we may learn to kill one another neatly and efficiently in our darkness. And there was no evening and no morning on the sixth day before the end.

And we said . . .

Let there be rockets and bombs to kill faster and easier; let there be gas chambers and furnaces to be more thorough. And there was no evening and no morning on the fifth day before the end.

And we said . . .

Let there be drugs and other forms of escape, for there is this constant annoyance — Reality — which is disturbing our comfort. And there was no evening and no morning on the fourth day before the end.

And we said . . .

Let there be divisions among the nations, so that we may know who is our common enemy. And there was no evening and no morning on the third day before the end.

And finally we said . . .

Let us create God in our image. Let some other God compete with us. Let us say that God thinks as we think, hates as we hate, and kills as we kill. And there was no morning and no evening on the second day before the end.

On the last day, there was a great noise on the face of the Earth. Fire consumed the beautiful globe, and there was silence. The blackened Earth now rested to worship the one true God; and God saw all that we had done, and in the silence over the smoldering ruins . . . God wept.

2. The fourth reader reads Romans 8:5-17.
3. The celebrant or deacon proclaims the Gospel reading, Luke 15:11-32, the Parable of the Prodigal Son. The celebrant

preaches a homily stressing the prodigality of the heavenly Father in his joyful, reconciling love for his alienated children.

4. The Prayers of the Faithful are recited, with special emphasis on the continued conversion of those who have been reconciled with the Trinity.

### The Liturgy of the Eucharist

1. All the lights are turned on as the canon of the Liturgy is now celebrated. If the celebrant is of the Roman Rite, Canon IV or the First Canon for Masses of Reconciliation would be appropriate. If the priest is of the Byzantine Rite, he will celebrate according to the Byzantine Rite of St. John Chrysostom.

2. There should be a procession of the gifts of bread and wine accompanied by the singing of an Offertory Hymn.

3. To prepare for the Eucharist, let the community join hands to sing together the Our Father, offering each other a sign of peace at its conclusion.

4. Holy Communion is given under both species, and a Communion Hymn is sung.

5. In the silent prayer following Communion, a meditation in honor of Mary, our heavenly Mother, could be read by a fifth reader. A suggestion would be "The Reed" by Caryll Houselander.

6. A concluding prayer and blessing is followed by a Recessional Hymn of joyful jubilation exalting God's goodness and our call to go forth to be instruments of his love and peace.

Chapter Nine

# THE SACRAMENT OF RECONCILIATION AMONG EASTERN ORTHODOX CHRISTIANS TODAY

## Orthodox Practice

In preceding chapters we have occasionally made reference to the Eastern Christian Churches and their approach to the Sacrament of Reconciliation. It is impossible to have an accurate idea of the administration of this sacrament simply from reading books by Orthodox writers. Practice often bears little relation to theory, as we have seen within the Roman Catholic Church. Also, practices differ among the various Orthodox Churches. Even now, both very rigorous and very lax approaches can be found and these often vary from priest to priest.[1]

We must keep in mind that the Roman Catholic Church has always recognized the validity of the seven sacraments of the Orthodox Churches, including their ordained priesthood. The Second Vatican Council reiterated this in its Decree on Eastern Catholic Churches:

> If any separated Eastern Christian should, under the guidance of the grace of the Holy Spirit, join himself to Catholic unity, no more should be required of him than

what a simple profession of the Catholic faith demands.
A valid priesthood is preserved among Eastern clerics.[2]

The first thing to observe is that Confession and the reception
of the Eucharist are usually rare events in the life of the average
Orthodox Christian. Yet, this was the case among Roman Catholics,
too, until the middle of the 19th century.

## Infrequent Reception of the Eucharist

Father Alexander Schmemann laments the infrequent reception of
Penance and the Eucharist among most Orthodox Christians:

> Why is it that for centuries nine out of ten Liturgies are
> being celebrated without communicants? And this pro-
> vokes no amazement, no trembling, whereas the desire
> to communicate more frequently, on the contrary, raises
> a real fear? How could the doctrine of once-a-year com-
> munion develop within the Church, the Body of Christ,
> as an accepted norm, a departure from which can be but
> an exception?[3]

He maintains that this infrequent reception of the Eucharist
came about out of a fear of receiving communion unworthily, of
profaning the Holy Mystery. Thus, we can see why the reception of
the Sacrament of Penance became infrequent with parishioners,
since there developed the practice of always confessing before
receiving Holy Communion. If the average Orthodox Christian
received the Eucharist once or twice a year, this meant that he or she
would also receive the Sacrament of Penance once or twice a year.

## The Minister of the Sacrament

Here we encounter a great difference between Russian and Greek
practice. All Orthodox Christians would agree that the priesthood

confers the power of absolution and that any priest, in case of emergency, can absolve. They would also agree that priests are required to have the proper authorization for the normal exercise of hearing confessions. Among the Russian and other Slav Orthodox, the parish priest normally is authorized to hear the confessions of the faithful. But in Greece, I found that many Orthodox parish priests, due to their low level of education (in poor mountainous areas some priests had never completed the eight elementary grades), were forbidden to hear confessions and to preach. On specific occasions, bishops would send into these areas priests properly educated to hear confessions. The shortage of authorized confessors would also account for the infrequency of receiving Holy Communion among these Orthodox faithful.

## Integrity of One's Confession

Among the Russian Orthodox it is expected that the penitent will, to the best of his or her ability, confess all sins great and small. This requirement indicates a realization on the part of all that the sacrament is not just an automatic prerequisite to receiving Communion. It is an exigency of the sacrament itself, which not only absolves one from sin but also provides a healing and curative balm for the soul. Thus, the priest and the penitent do not make the same distinction between mortal and venial sins as Roman Catholics habitually do. There is an accepted difference between serious sins and lighter ones, yet sin is essentially one and the same thing in all cases. It darkens the mind, weakens the will, and puts one in danger of an impenitent death. Hence it needs to be forgiven and to have its roots healed. The Orthodox penitent must confess all failures so the confessor can know his or her existential state in order to prescribe an effective remedy for reform.

*Different Forms of Celebration Within the Community*

Communal celebration of the Sacrament of Penance is the norm in the Christian East, and has been from the earliest centuries. Nonetheless, individual confession and absolution (Form I among Roman Catholics), communal celebration with individual confession and absolution (Form II), as well as communal celebration with general absolution (Form III) are all familiar to the various Eastern Churches.

The rite of private confession in all Byzantine Churches generally consists of the following acts: an opening prayer of praise; a litany with petitions for peace, salvation, and forgiveness of sins; a commemoration of Mary and praise to the Trinity; a prayer addressed to Christ asking forgiveness of sins; the Lord's Prayer; recitation of Psalm 51; a plea for mercy reminding God that his people are in need of pardon; confession of sins; a dialogue between the confessor and the penitent; and dismissal with a short prayer.

This rite offers freedom to the confessor to adapt it to the need of the individual penitent. In the Greek Church, the penitent and the priest are seated in an open area of the church or chapel and the whole rite takes place in the form of a friendly conversation. Having said this, we must admit, however, that there is hardly any auricular confession in Greek Orthodox parish churches today. The norm now is to provide general absolution to the whole community desiring to be reconciled to God.

*Communal Reconciliation Service and General Absolution*

Today there are found two great divergent views in the actual practice of the Sacrament of Penance. Among the Greek Churches in Greece and also in America, absolution is given without any confession whatever. I have witnessed this in Thessalonica before the great Feast of the Assumption of Our Lady, August 15. Before the priest brought the Eucharist to the parishioners, he invited those who wished to be reconciled to come forward. The penitents approached the priest with bowed heads. They struck their breasts, and in other gestures manifested to both priest and congregation their sorrow for their sins and their desire to be reconciled to both God and neighbor.

The priest then read aloud the following prayer:

Lord Jesus Christ, the Son of the living God, the Shepherd and Lamb who takes away the sin of the world, who forgave the loan to the two debtors and granted remission of her sins to the woman caught in adultery; do you yourself, O Lord, loose, remit, forgive the sins, the transgressions and the errors, both voluntary and involuntary, known or unknown, which have been committed through the violation and disobedience of these your servants.

And if they, being human, bearing flesh and dwelling in the world, were deceived in anything by the Devil, either in word or deed, knowingly or unknowingly, if they broke the word of a priest, or came under the curse of a priest, or fell under their own anathema, or have broken any oath, do you, the same good and forgiving Master, be pleased to set free these your servants by your word, granting them forgiveness from their own anathema and oath, according to your great mercy.

Yes, Master, Lord and Lover of mankind, hear us as we pray to your goodness for these your servants, and, in your great mercy, overlook all their faults; deliver them from eternal punishment; for you have said, O Master: "Whatever you pronounce unforgiven on earth shall remain unforgiven in heaven, and whatever you forgive on earth shall be forgiven in heaven." For you alone are without sin and to you we ascribe glory, together with your beginningless Father, and your all-holy and good and life-giving Spirit, now and for ever, and to the ages of ages. Amen.

117

There are a number of Orthodox pastors and liturgists who lament such a general absolution as well as those private confessions made to a priest only in the vaguest and most general of terms, such as, "Father, I am a great sinner, the greatest of sinners!"

Because of his own concern, Father Alexander Schmemann prepared a document for the Holy Synod of Bishops of the Orthodox Church in America (OCA) in February of 1972 on the subject of the practice of General Confession. Recognizing that "an overwhelming majority of the Church's members do not know either what Confession is or how to approach it,"[3] he set forth the following guidelines:

1. As a rule, General Confession is to be held in the evening after the evening service. Anyone who desires to receive Holy Communion must come to church at least the evening before.
2. General Confession begins with the priest reading aloud the Prayers Before Confession. These prayers are an integral part of the sacrament.
3. After the prayers, the priest invites the faithful to repentance, and prays that God will grant the Spirit in Confession, the gift "to see one's own sins," without which a formal enumeration will produce no spiritual fruit.
4. Following this is the Confession proper, i.e., the enumeration *by the priest* of those acts, thoughts, and desires with which we often offend the holiness of God, the sanctity of our neighbor, and that of our own soul. And, inasmuch as the priest himself like any man standing before God knows all these sins and all that sinfulness to be also in himself, this enumeration will be informal but sincere and will be done with a "broken and contrite heart" on behalf of all the penitents rather than aimed at them. During this enumeration each one will privately acknowledge his or her own guilt and truly repent.
5. In conclusion, the priest will invite the penitents to direct their inner vision away from their own unworthiness to the

table of the Lord which awaits them, to God's mercy and love; he will encourage them to prepare their whole being to desire that Communion of which we are never worthy but which is always a gift to us.

6. Then the priest will ask all those who feel the need to add something because of any special burden on their conscience to move aside and to wait. The others will approach him, one by one, and the priest will read the prayer of absolution, covering their heads with the epitrahilion (the stole) and giving them the cross to kiss.

7. Finally, while all those who have been reconciled listen to the prayers before Communion, the priest will hear individually those who desire to approach him in private and absolve them.[4]

Thus we see the American Russian Church favoring a rite similar to Form II of the Roman Catholic Rite, that is, a communal penance service with private and personal confession to a priest on the part of those who need it. In Fr. Schmemann's words: "The whole point here is precisely that the General Confession is under no circumstances meant simply to replace individual confession; it is not and must not be a substitute."[5]

## Community Forgiveness

We find in the Russian Orthodox Church a deeply moving celebration which takes place on the evening of the First Sunday of Lent. It highlights the mutual asking of pardon for any offenses committed toward the priest or one's neighbors. In this way the Church vividly teaches Christians at the beginning of Lent that they must love and forgive one another if they wish God to forgive them and accept their penance during Lent. It begins after evening Vespers with the priest turning toward his parishioners, making a profound bow to the floor, and saying: "My brethren, forgive me if I have hurt or offended you in any way, for I am a sinner." The people respond: "May God forgive and have mercy on you."

Then one by one the people come up to the priest, asking his forgiveness in the same words. They kiss each other three times, on both cheeks and the lips. Thus, a line is formed and mutual forgiveness is exchanged by all. A warm human relationship develops and deep reconciliations are effected at the beginning of Lent.

## Conclusion

This brief presentation of the modern day Orthodox practice of the Sacrament of Reconciliation has revealed some venerable customs and approaches that are a part of the Christian tradition. We see in both Eastern and Western Churches a movement inspired by the Holy Spirit to celebrate the Sacrament of Reconciliation through the use of two main forms, namely, the communal penance service and private confession. In both forms, care must be taken to avoid any sense of routineness or magic which would preclude the possibility of the sacrament's achieving its full effect: reconciliation and ongoing conversion. The Magisterium has offered us these two forms as gifts to be developed and used according to the mind of the Church in order to attain the goal of this sacrament: healing and conversion through sincere repentance and humble sorrow for our sins, so that, with intense fervor, we may live as authentic children of God, loving the Holy Trinity with all our mind and heart and will and our neighbor as ourselves.

# NOTES

## Chapter One

[1] *Constitution on the Sacred Liturgy*, #72, in *The Documents of Vatican II*, p. 161, ed. by W.M. Abbott & J. Gallagher (NY: The Guild & America Press, 1966).
[2] Among the many excellent studies, see: E. Schillebeeckx: *Christ the Sacrament* (NY, 1963); K. Rahner: *The Church and the Sacraments* in the series, *Questiones Disputatae* (NY, 1963).
[3] See Ralph Kiefer & Frederick R. McManus: *The Rite of Penance: Commentaries*, Vol. I: *Understanding the Document* (Washington, D.C.: The Liturgical Conference, 1975).
[4] See John McIlhon & Tad Guzie: *The Forgiveness of Sin* (Chicago: The Thomas More Association, 1979), p. 122ff.
[5] Karl Menninger: *Whatever Became of Sin?* (NY: Hawthorn Books, Inc., 1973), p. 13.
[6] Karl Rahner, "Problems Concerning Confession," in *Theological Investigations*, Vol. 3, tr. by Karl-H. & Boniface Kruger (Baltimore: Helicon Press, 1967), p. 19.
[7] *Rite of Penance: Study Edition*, U.S. Catholic Conference (Publications Office, U.S. Catholic Conference, Washington, D.C., 1975), #16, p. 6.
[8] See the excellent treatment of this topic by Kenan B. Osborne, OFM: *Reconciliation and Justification* (NY / Mahwah, NJ: Paulist Press, 1990).
[9] *Rite of Penance*, op. cit., pp. 6-11.
[10] *The Constitution on the Sacred Liturgy*, op. cit., #27, p. 148.
[11] *Code of Canon Law*, Canon 959. Cf. K. Osborne, op. cit., pp. 210-212.
[12] Pope John Paul II: *Reconciliation & Penance* (Washington, D.C.: USCC, 1984), pp. 58-64.
[13] See Raymond Brown: *The Epistles of John* (Garden City, NY: Doubleday, 1982), pp. 615-617.
[14] Ladislaus Orsy, SJ: *The Evolving Church & the Sacrament of Penance* (Denville, NJ: Dimension Books, 1978), p. 50.

## Chapter Two

[1] *Declaration on the Relationship of the Church to Non-Christian Religions*, #2; ed. W.M. Abbott, op. cit., p. 662.
[2] Ibid., p. 18-19.
[3] See John Shea: *What a Modern Catholic Believes About Sin* (Chicago: Thomas More, 1971).

121

⁴ Cardinal John Henry Newman. Quoted in: *A New Catechism: Catholic Faith for Adults*; tr. by Kevin Smyth (NY: Herder & Herder, 1967), p. 261.

⁵ For a rather general summary of the topic of repentance, cf.: *The Encyclopedia of Religion*, Vol. 12, art. "Repentance," pp. 337-342, by David E. Aune. On the topic of confession among non-Christian religions, see op. cit., Vol. 4, art. "Confession," by Ugo Bianchi, pp. 1-7 (NY: Macmillan Publishing Co., 1987).

⁶ Article: "Repentance," in *The Encyclopedia of Religion*, art. cit., p. 337.

⁷ For a most complete treatment on the Jewish concept of repentance cf. Joseph B. Soloveitchik: *On Repentance*, ed. by Pinchas Peli (NY / Ramsey, NJ: Paulist Press, 1984).

⁸ On the Yom Kippur prayers, cf. Rabbi A.I. Kook: *The Lights of Repentance* (Jerusalem, 1970).

⁹ For a masterful presentation on *penthos* in the Old and New Testaments and the writings of the Fathers of the Desert, cf. I. Hausherr, SJ: *Penthos — La Doctrine de la compunction dans l'Orient chrétien* (Rome: Pontifical Oriental Institute, 1944) in *Orientalia Christiana Analecta Series*, no. 132.

¹⁰ Op. cit., p. 22.

¹¹ J.B. Soloveitchik, op. cit., p. 19.

¹² St. Augustine: *Enarrationes in Psalmos*, 74, *PL* (Patrologia Latina; Migne), Vol. 35, 953.

¹³ Cited in *The Fire and the Cloud: An Anthology of Catholic Spirituality*, ed. David A. Fleming, SM (NY: Paulist Press, 1978), p. 318.

## Chapter Three

¹ Joachim Jeremias: *New Testament Theology* (NY: Charles Scribners, 1971) tr. J. Bowden, pp. 76-121.

² See J.H. Charlesworth: *Jesus Within Judaism* (NY: Doubleday, 1988), p. 7ff. Cf. also Kenan B. Osborne, OFM: *Reconciliation and Justification*, op. cit., who also develops these four elements of the Gospel preaching of Jesus, pp. 29-37.

³ For a treatment of the meaning of the parables of Jesus, but especially that of the prodigal son, cf. Joachim Jeremias: *Rediscovering the Parables* (NY: Scribners, 1966), pp. 97-105; and Madeleine Boucher: *Parables* (Wilmington, DE: Michael Glazier, Inc., 1981).

⁴ See my book: *God's Incredible Mercy* (Staten Island, NY: Alba House, 1989), pp. 126-129.

⁵ See my book: *Uncreated Energy* (NY: Amity House, 1987).

⁶ For a good summary treatment of the emphasis on the death of Jesus on the cross to the neglect of the resurrection, cf. K. Osborne, op. cit., pp. 38-51.

⁷ *The Baltimore Catechism* (NY: Sadlier, 1941), p. 34.

⁸ F.X. Durwell, CSSR: *The Resurrection*, tr. Rosemary Sheed (NY: Sheed & Ward, 1966), pp. 149-150.

⁹ Yves Congar, OP: *Jesus Christ*, tr. Luke O'Neill (NY: Herder & Herder, 1966), pp. 193-194.

¹⁰ *Constitution on Divine Revelation*, #8; ed. W.M. Abbott, op. cit., p. 116.

¹¹ Ladislaus Orsy, SJ: *The Evolving Church and the Sacrament of Penance*, op. cit., p. 51.

# Chapter Four

[1] For some of the leading secondary sources that treat of the early Christian Churches' approach to the Sacrament of Penance, cf.: E. Amann: "Penitence," in *Dictionnaire de théologie catholique* (Paris: Letouzey et Ane; 1933), vol. 12; P. Anciaux: *The Sacrament of Penance* (NY: Sheed & Ward, 1962); E. Bourque: *Histoire de la Penitence-Sacrement* (Quebec: Laval Univ. Press, 1947); H. von Campenhausen: *Ecclesiastical Authority and Spiritual Power in the Church of the First Three Centuries* (Stanford, CA: Stanford Univ. Press, 1969), tr. J.A. Baker; J. Dallen: *The Reconciling Community: The Rite of Penance* (NY: Pueblo, 1986); J.A. Favazza: *The Order of Penitents* (Collegeville, MN: The Liturgical Press, 1987); P. Baltier: *L'Église et la remission des péchés aux premiers siécles* (Paris: Beaushesne, 1932); L. Hamelin: *Reconciliation in the Church*, tr. M. O'Connell (Collegeville, MN: The Liturgical Press, 1980); L. Orsy: *The Evolving Church and the Sacrament of Penance* (Denville, NJ: Dimension Books, 1978); B. Poschmann: *Penance and the Anointing of the Sick*, tr. F. Courtney (NY: Herder & Herder, 1963); _____: *Penitentia Secunda* (Bonn: Peter Hanstein, 1940); K. Rahner: "Penance in the Early Church" in *Theological Investigations*, Vol. 15 (NY: Crossroad, 1982), tr. Lionel Swain; H. Swete: "Penitential Discipline in the First Three Centuries" in *Journal of Theological Studies* (London: 1903), No. 4, pp. 321-337; Oscar D. Watkins: *A History of Penance, Being a Study of the Authorities*, Vol. A: *The Whole Church to A.D. 450*, and Vol. B: *The Western Church from A.D. 450 to A.D. 1215* (London: Longmans Green & Co., 1920).

[2] Cf. A. Lefevre: "Péché et pénitence dans la Bible," in *La Maison-Dieu* (Paris, 1958), Vol. 55, pp. 8-13.

[3] Cf. J. Murphy-O'Connor: "Péché et communauté dans le Nouveau Testament," in *Revue biblique* (Paris, 1967), Vol. 74, pp. 161-193.

[4] Cf. Raymond Brown: *The Gospel According to John* (Garden City, NY: Doubleday & Co., 1970), Vol. 2, p. 1044; B. Rigaux: "'Lier et delier'. Les ministeres de reconciliation dans l'Église des temps apostoliques," in *La Maison-Dieu*, Vol. 117 (1974), pp. 86-135; A. Nocent: "Il sacramento della penitenza e della riconciliazione," in *I Sacramenti: teologia e storia della celebrazione* (Genoa: Marietti, 1986), pp. 133-203.

[5] R. Brown, op. cit., p. 1044.

[6] Cf. J.A. Favazza, op. cit., p. 81.

[7] Cf. José Ramos-Regidor: "'Reconciliation' in the Primitive Church and Its Lessons for Theological and Pastoral Practice Today," in *Concilium*, ed. E. Schillebeeckx (NY: Paulist Press, 1971), Vol. 61: *Sacramental Reconciliation*, p. 77 ff.

[8] Cf. A. Nocent, op. cit., p. 133ff.

[9] Op. cit., p. 70.

[10] K. Rahner, op. cit., p. 18.

[11] *Didache*, tr. O.D. Watkins, Vol. A., pp. 73-74, op. cit. For patristic citations, I will rely on this work of Watkins. Another source of texts on Penance from the early Church to more recent times that I have found helpful is the collection of texts by Paul F. Palmer, SJ: *Sources of Christian Theology*, Vol. 2: *Sacraments and Forgiveness* (Westminster, MD: Newman, 1959).

[12] *First Letter of St. Clement to the Corinthians*, tr. Watkins, op. cit., p. 72.

[13] Poschmann believes that this is the only use of the word *exomologesis* by

Clement where the confession of sin is explicitly meant. Cf. his *Penance and Anointing of the Sick*: PAS, op. cit., p. 22, ftnote. 23.
[14] Watkins, p. 73. St Ignatius: *To the Philadelphians*, 8.
[15] St. Polycarp: *To the Philippians*; 5, 1: Watkins, p. 73.
[16] For a detailed analysis of Hermas' *The Shepherd* and English translation see C. Taylor: *The Shepherd of Hermas* (London: SPCK, 1903-06), 2 vols. We need not dwell on any elements but Hermas' teaching on penance and reconciliation.
[17] Cf. Johannes Quasten: *Patrology*, Vol. 1 (Westminster, MD: Newman, 1951), pp. 97-98; Mandate 4, 3, 1-6.
[18] Ibid., pp. 98-99.
[19] For an English translation, cf. C. Dodgson: *Library of the Fathers*, Vol. 10 (Oxford, 1842), pp. 349-369; also W. LeSaint: *Tertullian on Penance: On Penance and Purity* in *Ancient Christian Writers*, Vol. 28 (Westminster, MD).
[20] English translation, cf. S. Thelwall in *Ante-Nicene Christian Library* (Edinburgh, 1888), Vol. 18, pp. 56-122.
[21] LeSaint, op. cit., pp. 219-220, n. 193.
[22] Ibid., 9, 3-4, pp. 31-32.
[23] Cyprian, Letter 14: *To the Presbyters and Deacons Functioning in Rome*, 2, PL 4, 486 A-B.
[24] Ibid., Letter 17: *PL* 4, 277 A.
[25] Oscar D. Watkins: *A History of Penance, Being a Study of the Authorities*, Vol. A: *The Whole Church to A.D. 450* (London, 1920).
[26] Ibid., pp. 460-465.
[27] Ibid.

## Chapter Five

[1] Orsy, op. cit. "Surprisingly enough, there were two distinct points of departure: one, right from the beginning, in the churches around the Mediterranean; the other, from the fifth century, in the churches in Ireland" (p. 30).
[2] Kathleen Hughes: "The Celtic Church and the Papacy," in *The English Church and the Papacy in the Middle Ages* (NY: University Press, 1965), ed. C.H. Lawrence, pp. 16-17.
[3] J.T. McNeill and Helena M. Gamer: *Medieval Handbooks of Penance* (NY: Columbia University Press, 1938), pp. 44-46.
[4] Cf. G. Maloney, SJ: *Pilgrimage of the Heart* (San Francisco: Harper & Row, 1983), pp. 18ff.
[5] McNeill and Gamer, op. cit., pp. 44-46.
[6] Cf. G. Maloney, SJ: "The Elder of the Christian East as Spiritual Leader, " in *Studies in Formative Spirituality* (Duquesne, PA: Duquesne University Press, 1982), pp. 75-87.
[7] See Casmir Kucharek: *The Sacramental Mysteries — A Byzantine Approach* (Allendale, NJ: Alleluia Press, 1976), p. 238.
[8] C. Kucharek writes, "Vestiges of the old system, however, are seen in the Nomocanons or *Kanonaria* (8th to 15th centuries) which the priest used for questioning the penitent, selecting the correct *epitimia* or penance, and imparting the proper forms of absolution" (p. 238).
[9] Cf. H. von Campenhausen: "The Ascetic Idea of Exile and Medieval Monasti-

cism," in *Tradition and Life in the Church* (Philadelphia: Fortress, 1968), tr. A.V. Littledale.

10 Cf. Osborne, op. cit., pp. 88ff.

11 See the texts given by Watkins, Vol. B: *The Western Church from A.D. 450 to 1215*, op. cit., pp. 628-630.

12 Ibid., Vol. B, pp. 585-87.

13 See the texts found in Paul F. Palmer, op. cit., Vol. II, pp. 145-152.

14 Text cited by K. Osborne, op. cit., p. 91.

15 Ibid.

16 Translation found in Palmer, op. cit., pp. 197-198.

17 Cf. A. Teetaert: *La Confession aux laiques dans l'Église Latine* (Paris: J. Gabalda, 1926).

18 There was no unanimity among the scholastic theologians of this period on the question of the sacramentality of confession to a priest and the non-sacramentality of confession to lay persons. It was Duns Scotus who made the strongest and most powerful argument against the sacramentality of a confession made to a lay person.

19 P. Adnes: *La Penitencia* (Madrid: La Editorial Catolica, 1981), p. 184.

20 Trent, 14, 5. Even our daily sins can be remitted by many different means, especially the Eucharist (Trent, 13, 2).

21 K. Rahner: "The Meaning of Frequent Confession of Devotion," in *Theological Investigations* (Baltimore: Helicon Press, 1967), Vol. 3, p. 186.

22 Cf. K. Osborne, op. cit., pp. 196-197 and 198-200.

23 Cf. J. Dallen: *The Reconciling Community: The Rite of Penance* (NY: Pueblo, 1986), pp. 180-193.

## Chapter Six

1 J. Dallen, op. cit., p. 193.

2 Cf. K. Osborne, op. cit., pp. 198-200.

3 Ibid., p. 199.

4 *Constitution on the Sacred Liturgy*, #72, ed. W.M. Abbott, p. 161.

5 Ibid., No. 109, p. 170.

6 Ibid., No. 34, p. 149. Cf. also No. 24, p. 147.

7 Ibid., No 35, p. 149.

8 Ibid., No. 27, p. 148.

9 Ibid., No. 26, p. 147.

10 *Constitution on the Church*, No. 11, p. 28.

11 Summarized from the *National Bulletin on Liturgy*, Canadian Catholic Conference, 9 (1976), p. 13.

12 For the contents and commentaries on these rites, I have used the English translation: *New Rite of Penance: Commentaries*, Vol. I: *Understanding the Document*, ed. R. Keifer and F.R. McManus; Vol. II: *Implementing the Rite*, ed. E. McMahon-Jeep; Vol. III: *Background and Directions*, ed. N. Mitchell (Washington, D.C.: The Liturgical Conference, 1978).

13 F. Sottocornola and P. Jounel, who had been among the leading theologians who drafted the new rite document, complained of this omission. Cf. F. Sottocornola: *A Look at the New Rite of Penance* (Washington, D.C.: USCC, 1975), tr. T.

Krosnicki, p. 67; P. Jounel: "La Liturgie de la reconciliation," in *La Maison-Dieu*, Vol. 117 (1974), p. 9.
14  No. 35, p. 149.
15  *Constitution on the Church (Lumen Gentium)*, No. 11, p. 28.
16  *Constitution on the Sacred Liturgy*, No. 27, p. 148.
17  Sacred Congregation for the Doctrine of the Faith: *Normae Pastorales*: *Sacramentum paenitentiae*, 64, *AAS* (1972), pp. 510-514.

## Chapter Seven

1  National Conference of Catholic Bishops: *The Church at Prayer. A Holy Temple of the Lord* (Washington, D.C.: United States Catholic Conference, 1983), No. 27, p. 14.
2  *Sacramentum paenitentiae* in *AAS* 64 (1972), pp. 510-514. An English translation can be found in *Penance and Reconciliation in the Church*. Liturgy Documentary Series, No. 7 (Washington, D.C.: USCC, 1986), pp. 31-35.
3  Cf. K. Osborne, op. cit., pp. 222-227.
4  For Pope Paul VI's allocution of 1978 cf. *AAS* 70 (1978), p. 330.
5  John Paul II: *Reconciliation and Penance: Post-Synodal Apostolic Exhortation of John Paul II to the Bishops, Clergy and Faithful on Reconciliation and Penance in the Mission of the Church Today* (Washington, D.C.: USCC, 1984), No. 31, I, p. 115.
6  Ibid., p. 128.
7  Tad Guzie, op. cit., pp. 153-154.
8  *AAS* 64 (1972), pp. 513-514.
9  Cf. my booklet on a daily examination of conscience: *Goodnight, Lord. Healing the Day's Hurts* (Seal Beach, CA: Contemplative Ministries Press, 1983).
10  Pope Pius X: *Quam singulari* in *AAS* 2 (1910), pp. 577-583.
11  Cf. L. Gaupin: "Let those who have faith not be hasty: Penance and Children," in *Reconciliation. The Continuing Agenda* (Collegeville, MN: The Liturgical Press, 1987), ed. R.J. Kennedy, pp. 219-238.

## Chapter Eight

1  Frans Heggen: "The Service of Penance: A Description and Appreciation of Some Models," in *Concilium*, ed. E. Schillebeeckx, Vol. 61: *Sacramental Reconciliation* (NY: Herder, 1971), pp. 134ff. Cf. also, *Constitution on the Sacred Liturgy*, op. cit., #27.
2  Cf. *Constitution on the Sacred Liturgy*, #24, 26, 27, 33, 34, 35, and 109; *Constitution on the Church*, #11; and *Decree on the Ministry of Priests*, #5; op. cit.
3  F. Sottocornola: *A Look at the New Rite of Penance*, op. cit., p. 3.
4  G. Dieckmann, OSB: "The Laying on of Hands," in *Proceedings of the Catholic Theological Society of America*, Vol. 29 (1974), p. 350.
5  *The New Rite of Penance*, op. cit., #45.
6  Ibid., #22.

## Notes

# Chapter Nine

[1] Various authors have written about the unique approaches in the history and present practices of the Eastern Churches. Cf. L. Ligier: "Le Sacrement de Penitence selon la Tradition orientale," in *Nouvelle Revue Theologique*, Vol. 89 (1967), pp. 940-967; Ibid., "Dimension personnelle et dimension communitarian de Penitence en Orient," in *La Maison-Dieu*, Vol. 90 (1967), pp. 155-188; P. Kikolasch: "The Sacrament of Penance: Learning from the East," in *Concilium*, Vol 61 (1971), op. cit., pp. 65-75; E. Hermann: "Il piu antico penitenziale greco," in *Orientale Christiana Periodica* (Rome, 1952), Vol. 19, pp. 71-127; H.I. Dalmais: "Le Sacrement de penitence chez les Orientaux," in *La Maison-Dieu*, Vol. 56 (1958), pp. 22-29.

[2] *Decree on the Eastern Catholic Churches*, op. cit., #25, p. 383.

[3] Fr. Alexander Schmemann: *Report to the Orthodox Church of America* (OCA) Synod (1973); *On Communal Penance Service*, p. 7.

[4] Ibid., pp. 15-17.

[5] Ibid., p. 17.